4/04

£4.99

Documents and Debates
Nineteenth—Century Britain

Documents and Debates
General Editor: John Wroughton M.A., F.R.Hist.S.

Nineteenth-Century Britain

Richard Brown
Houghton Regis Upper School, Bedfordshire
Christopher Daniels
Royal Latin School, Buckingham

M
MACMILLAN

FOR OUR PARENTS

First published 1980
Reprinted 1981, 1982, 1983, 1984, 1985, 1986, 1989

Published by
MACMILLAN EDUCATION LTD
Houndmills, Basingstoke, Hampshire RG21 2XS
and London
Companies and representatives
throughout the world

Printed in Hong Kong

British Library Cataloguing in Publication Data
Daniels, Christopher
Nineteenth century Britain. — (Documents and debates).
1. Great Britain — History — 19th century
I. Brown, Richard   II. Series
941.97   DA530
ISBN 0—333—24574—1

Contents

941.081
NIN
1980

General Editor's Preface   vii

Acknowledgements   viii

The Nineteenth Century   1

I   The Question of 'Toryism' 1815—27   7

II   The Reform Act of 1832   17

III   The New Poor Law   28

IV   Chartism   41

V   Peel — A Question of Motivation   49

VI   The Transition to Democracy 1846—68   59

VII   Foreign Policy 1812—65   70

VIII   Egypt and the 'Scramble for Africa'   81

IX   Victorian Trilogy   89

X   The Liberal Welfare Reforms   100

General Editor's Preface

This book forms part of a series entitled *Documents and Debates*, which is aimed primarily at the sixth form. Each volume covers approximately one century of either British or European history and consists of up to ten sections, each dealing with a major theme. In most cases a varied selection of documents will bring evidence to bear on the chosen theme, supplemented by a stimulating extract from a modern historian. A few 'Debate' sections, however, will centre on the most important controversies of each century. Here extracts from the changing opinions of modern research, normally found only in learned journals and expensive monographs, will be made available in manageable form. The series intends partly to provide experience for those pupils who are required to answer questions on documentary extracts at 'A' Level, and partly to provide pupils of all abilities with a digestible and interesting collection of source material, which will extend the normal textbook approach.

This book is designed essentially for the pupil's own personal use. The author's introduction will put the century as a whole into perspective, highlighting the central issues, main controversies, available source material and recent developments. Although it is clearly not our intention to replace the traditional textbook, each section will carry its own brief introduction, which will set the documents into context. The short, select bibliography is intended to encourage the pupil to follow up issues raised in the section by further reading – without being subjected to the off-putting experience of an exhaustive list. A wide variety of source material has been used in order to give the pupils the maximum amount of experience – letters, speeches, newspapers, memoirs, diaries, official papers, Acts of Parliament, Minute Books, accounts, local documents, family papers, etc. The questions vary in difficulty, but aim throughout to compel the pupil to think in depth by the use of unfamiliar material. Historical knowledge and understanding will be tested, as well as basic comprehension. Pupils will also be encouraged by the questions to assess the reliability of evidence, to recognise bias and emotional prejudice, to reconcile conflicting accounts and to extract the essential from the irrelevant. Some questions, marked with an asterisk, require knowledge outside the immediate extract and are intended for further research or discussion, based on the pupil's general knowledge of the period. Finally, we hope that students using this material will learn something of the nature of historical inquiry and the role of the historian.

John Wroughton

Acknowledgements

The authors and publishers wish to thank the following who have kindly given permission for the use of copyright material:—

Associated Book Publishers Ltd for extracts from *Disraeli* by Robert Blake, published by Eyre & Spottiswoode (Publishers) Ltd, and *The Making of Victorian England* by G. Kitson Clark, published by Methuen & Co. Ltd;

Ernest Benn Ltd for extracts from *History of the English People in the Nineteenth Century*, vol. 3, 'Triumph of Reform' by E. Halévy translated by E. I. Watkin;

Frank Cass & Co. Ltd for extracts from *Lord Liverpool and Liberal Toryism* by W. R. Brock; *Foundations of British Foreign Policy 1792–1902*, edited by Temperley and Penson (1966), and *European Imperialism and the Partition of Africa*, edited by E. F. Penrose (1975);

Chatto & Windus Ltd for extracts from *Queen Victoria* by L. Strachey;

The Controller of Her Majesty's Stationery Office for extracts from *Hansard*, 3rd Series 1846;

Dobson Books Ltd for extracts from *Bagehot's Historical Essays*, edited, with an Introduction by Norman St John-Stevas;

Gerald Duckworth & Co. Ltd for an extract from *Peel* by G. Kitson Clark;

European Journal of Sociology, II (1961) for extracts from *A Welfare State*;

Hamlyn Publishing Group for an extract from *Liberalism and the Social Problem* by W. S. Churchill;

Augustus M. Kelley, New Jersey, for an extract from *History, Gazeteer and Directory of Suffolk* by William White.

Longman Group Ltd for extracts from *British History in the Nineteenth Century and After* by G. M. Trevelyan, and *Studies in the Theory of Imperialism* by R. Owen and B. Sutcliffe;

Melbourne University Press for extracts from *The Making of the Second Reform Bill* by Dr. F. B. Smith

John Murray (Publishers) Ltd for an extract from *Gladstone* by Phillip Magnus;

Thomas Nelson & Sons Ltd for an extract from *From Castlereagh to Gladstone 1815–1885* by D. Beale;

Oxford University Press for extracts from *Corn, Cash, Commerce* by Boyd Hilton;

Penguin Books Ltd for extracts from *The History Primer* by J. H. Hexter (Allen Lane 1972) Copyright © 1971 Basic Books Inc.

Routledge & Keegan Paul Ltd for an extract from *The Reluctant Imperialists* by C. J. Lowe;

The Joseph Rowntree Charitable Trust for an extract from *Poverty, A Study of Town Life* by Seebohm Rowntree;

Scottish Academic Press Ltd for an extract from *Lord Liverpool's Administration 1815–1822* by J. E. Cookson;

Cover Mansell Collection

Every effort has been made to trace all the copyright holders but if any have been inadvertently overlooked the publishers will be pleased to make the necessary arrangement at the first opportunity.

The authors would also like to thank the Bodleian Library, Oxford; Bolton Public Library and Dunstable Public Library for their assistance.

The Nineteenth Century

Evidence and the Historian

Very few persons alive today will leave behind them when they die, any direct record whatever of any sound they uttered or any bodily movement they made, save, perhaps, as a voice and a speck in a roaring crowd. And finally, no men or women in the entire past up to the 1880's left any audible record whatever of any sound they ever made; no men or women up to the 1890's left behind any direct visual record of a gesture, a change of a facial expression, a bodily movement. For any dates earlier than those, we have to rely on still pictures and portraits to judge what any man looked like and on the pitifully ill-adapted rhetoric of written language to hazard a guess at what he sounded like . . . . Historians cannot too frequently remind themselves that their material is not the enormously dense networks of actual human relations in the past, but only the fragmented surviving record from which they may be able to elicit some sense of some of the intelligible patterns and structures that once were part of that network. (J. H. Hexter.)

As this collection of documents is a selection, it is advisable to indicate that it consists exclusively of written or printed sources, and a whole range of evidential material (pictures, cartoons, buildings, oral evidence) has not been included. As the writing of history involves selecting evidence this is inevitable, but the reader should ask why these ten themes have been chosen, why certain documents within these themes have been selected, and whether this choice and editing of documents affects the evidence and the conclusions that can be drawn from it. As G. Kitson Clark wrote,

. . . to be significant history must choose from the mass of the records of what has happened those facts which relate to a particular issue or group of issues or which gain their meaning from a particular calculus of values. And there is no reason why these reference points should be the same for all individuals in all generations.

The distinction between 'facts' and 'evidence' is fundamental: consider this passage from *What is History?* by E. H. Carr.

Let us take a look at the process by which a mere fact about the past is transformed into a fact of history. At Stalybridge Wakes in 1850, a vendor of gingerbread, as the result of some petty dispute, was deliberately kicked to death by an angry mob. Is this a fact of history? A year ago I should unhesitatingly have said 'no'. It was recorded by an eye-witness in some little-known memoirs [Lord George Sanger, *Seventy Years a Showman*]; but I had never seen it judged worthy of mention by any historian. A year ago Dr Kitson Clark cited it in his Ford lectures in Oxford. Does this make it into a historical fact? Not, I think, yet. Its present status, I suggest, is that it has been proposed for membership of the select club of historical facts. It now awaits a seconder and sponsors. It may be that in the course of the next few years we shall see this fact appearing first in footnotes, then in the text, of articles and books about nineteenth-century England, and that in twenty or thirty years' time it may be a well-established historical fact. Alternatively, nobody may take it up, in which case it will relapse into the limbo of unhistorical facts about the past from which Dr Kitson Clark has gallantly attempted to rescue it. What will decide which of these two things will happen? It will depend, I think, on whether the thesis or interpretation in support of which Dr Kitson Clark cited this incident is accepted by other historians as valid and significant. Its status as a historical fact will turn on a question of interpretation. This element of interpretation enters into every fact of history.

The event is undoubtedly based on evidence and unless Lord George Sanger can be shown to have been an unreliable witness this incident is likely to be true. (It could, perhaps, be checked in other contemporary sources.) It is evidence. Whether it be 'accepted' seems irrelevant, as the event has an existence as evidence quite distinct from whether it is well-known, or well-established, or whether it fits a particular interpretation. If the event is based on verifiable sources then it becomes a fact of history. Only if the source of our information were dubious, or alternative evidence produced which contradicted Sanger's story, would we reduce the event as cited by Sanger to 'evidence' rather than 'fact'. In that case it would be a valid question to ask why Sanger put down what he believed to be true when other sources were different from his, or why he chose to write an inaccurate account, knowing it to be so. Carr's distinction is true to the extent that the historian is concerned to make sense of the past, or, as Hexter wrote, 'the surviving records of the past are a set of dimensionless points. As such they lie outside history. It is the work of historians to draw lines connecting records of the past, [and thus bring the] dimensionless points within the dimension of history.'

The French historian Marc Bloch wrote that 'a document is a witness; and like most witnesses it rarely speaks until one begins to question it'. To know what questions to ask of source material is to become involved in what has been described as the 'public tradition of inquiry', where documents and debates are set in a context of knowing the state of historical research on a topic. There is a paradox here, because detailed knowledge of a past society, involving knowing and understanding the range of source material available for study of that society, depends on using evidence in the first place. Use of this evidence then adds to knowledge of the society in question. There is no distinction between 'content' and 'method' in history. Can the student then participate in this 'public tradition of inquiry' as his knowledge of a period of history will be much less than that of an academic historian? The answer is yes. Without initiation into the problems and opportunities of using evidence and writing history, the student's understanding of the subject will be stunted:

processes are as important as products. Hence the open-ended nature of the section on the New Poor Law, where evidence (admittedly pre-selected) is presented and open to various uses. The validity of completed work on this section depends on how the evidence has been used, what questions have been raised and resolved or left for lack of further information, and on how credible the written end—product is. Part of this section offers the tantalising opportunity of writing history from evidence provided, without the usual constraints of a specific essay title, or notes on a particular topic. The sources of this section will not provide the answers to many questions on workhouse life or the 1834 Poor Law in action, but they may stimulate questions like 'What categories of people were in the workhouse?', 'Where were they from?'

Local history is playing an increasing role in sixth-form history, especially in examination projects, and several sections could form the basis of research in a library or record office on the similarities and differences between the local and national record, and between different regions.

In conclusion, a vital, if often forgotten, aspect of the relationship between the historian and his sources is what Hexter called the 'second record'.

> It is everything he can bring to bear on the record of the past in order to elicit from that record the best account he can render of what he believes actually happened in the past. Potentially, therefore, it embraces his skills, the range of his knowledge, the set of his mind, the substance, quality and character of his experience — his total consciousness. Since no historian is identical with any other historian, what each historian brings, his second record, differs in some measure from the second record of every other historian. . . . History, therefore, depends not only on the surviving record of the past but on what historians bring to it. And all any historian brings to the first record lies somewhere in his second record. Every time a historian moves explicitly or implicitly from the record of the past to a historical assertion *about* the past he is drawing on his second record, claiming that he has and, if necessary, can produce from his second record grounds for his assertion that the first record means what he says it means. In this way he makes some part of his second record, hitherto private and inaccessible, public and accessible, open to criticism and evaluation.

The 'second record' exists at all levels of study, but if it is not brought into play in a conscious way, work on historical sources will offer very little. Our knowledge of people benefits our study of the past, and the understanding of what it was like to be someone different from us in the past is of value in the present and future. Perhaps the most important source lies not in this book but in the 'second record' of each reader of it.

Nineteenth-Century Britain

The phenomenon which historians call the 'industrial revolution' dominates any consideration of the nineteenth and early twentieth century. The most important features of these were demographic growth from the 1750s with the expansion of the population of England and Wales by twenty millions between 1801 and 1901, the expansion of the textile industry and its gradual removal northwards with its stimulating effects on the economy as a whole and the increased productivity of agriculture. These factors together made a radical rethinking of the position of man (particularly the 'common man') in society possible or even inevitable. The sections in this book are concerned with this change in accent and emphasis; specifically, they deal with the response of the representatives of pre-industrial political society, the aristocratic élite, to pressure from outside their political framework and understanding and to the political problems thrown up in the volcanic actions of industrialisation. Space has not allowed us to consider this process from every viewpoint. We are painfully aware of the lack of consideration given to the Celtic fringe, the problems of religion and to the intellectual ferment of the nineteenth century, all of which played an important part in the change from an oligarchic to a democratic conception of society.

In 1812 British society was governed by the members of a small aristocratic élite whose power and authority was based on their possession of upwards of fifty per cent of all agricultural land and the 'influence' which this gave them over the rest of society. Britain had not undergone a political revolution in the late eighteenth century — much of society believed that because of the paternalistic attitude of the aristocratic élite, that élite should continue to rule. This was an attitude that implied some degree of social responsibility by the élite for the life of the rest of society and the existence of some social mobility based on service and talent. The political issues that arose in late eighteenth- and early nineteenth-century society may have been cloaked in the garb of ideology but they were essentially pragmatic responses by different sections of society to the specific problems facing them. Historians differ over whether the idea of 'political party' existed at all at this time, but there existed nothing comparable to the notion of 'party' which evolved in the late nineteenth century. Connection, family groupings and personality played a vital role. Pragmatism not ideology was the key to political understanding. Though the existing political system was attacked as unfair and unrepresentative — which by modern standards it certainly was — it still had considerable support from the county landed interests in the 1780s and among the urban artisans in the 1790s. This was in contrast to its French counterpart which was completely devastated by 1789. The political system which underpinned the aristocratic élite in Britain was based upon 'balance' and 'harmony'. While these ideas were acceptable to the bulk of society, and while the aristocratic élite remained a credible governing body, there would be no 'fundamental' change which that élite did not itself originate.

The long ministry of Lord Liverpool from 1812 to 1827 saw the end of this finely-balanced system. The political implications of industrialisation began to be felt. Luddism, the impact of proletarian radicalism between 1816 and 1819, the crisis in agriculture from 1811 and the increasing polarisation between industry and agriculture (north and south), all placed pressures of an intensity not experienced before upon government. Liverpool's response was as pragmatic as Pitt's had been in the 1790s. Yet, as section I shows, Liverpool's ministry is best understood not in terms of liberalism and conservatism but of the relationship between 'economic' and 'political' versions of Toryism. 'Fundamental' reform did not occur but there were significant tinkerings with the economic basis of the existing political system, tinkerings though which could not delay for long its political transformation.

What Asa Briggs sees as 'the period of flux' (between Liverpool's seizure in February 1827 and the formation of a Whig government in November 1830) may be seen as the crisis which ended government of the 'Old Style'. It saw the opening attacks on the fundamentals of the 'Constitution'. The 1830 election may not have been decisive in any specific sense but it did open the way for the Whigs, who, unlike the Tories, believed in fundamental political reform. The passage of parliamentary reform in 1832, the Municipal Corporation Act of 1835 and the Whigs' innovative reforms on major questions raised or accentuated by industrialisation laid the foundations of nineteenth-century government and administration. The Poor Law reforms of the 1830s exemplify this. The failure of Peel as a viable parliamentary leader after 1846 was his failure to appreciate the significance these changes had in parliament. The aristocratic élite survived largely unaltered – except that it showed a real flexibility in its willingness to accept, albeit grudgingly, the expanding middle class. Peel's tragedy was that although he appreciated this and showed a desire to act pragmatically to give the middle class further reforms, parliament had become a more ideological body with an intense suspicion, if not downright hatred of pragmatism. The failure of Chartism was the failure of the working class to organise nationally and so provide a unified alternative to the aristocratic élite and its allies who were still able to cry 'revolution' and thus rally much of the nation behind them.

'Influence' remained important from 1846 until the passage of reform in 1867. In many ways the eighteenth-century idea of government made a revival, caused largely by the reorientation of political groupings in parliament and the final emergence of a modern party structure. There was no further 'fundamental' reform – only an extension and expansion of ideas which originated between 1830 and 1846. Palmerston reigned supreme and the ghost of Peel haunted politics; it was not until the former's death in October 1865 that any further reform came. It was the reform agitation of 1866–7 which saw Parliament and the aristocratic élite accept that a proportion of the working class could safely be given the vote. This was an achievement for which Disraeli, Gladstone and the middle and working classes all claimed credit.

In 1867 came political acceptance of the increasingly urban nature of British society and the aristocratic élite forced to rethink its position. (The individual living in a rural area had to wait until 1884 to obtain the vote because the conservatism of the élite remained stronger there.) Political party, exemplified by the relationship between Gladstone and Disraeli from 1868 to 1881, and the developing national and local organisation of Conservatism and Liberalism became dominant. Ideology became an acceptable part of the British political system. The aristocratic élite remained, in a modified form, but it had to accept that 'party' and class interest were increasingly relevant and necessary in a society in which the problems created by industrialisation had not yet been fully resolved. These problems were increasingly discussed after 1880 when the economic benefits of industrial development began to look more questionable. The work of Booth and Seebohm Rowntree reinforced this awareness of the difficulties and the Liberal reforms from 1906 attempted to solve them.

Political change in the nineteenth century occurred slowly despite the extra-parliamentary forces arraigned against the old pre-industrial élitist system. The changes that did occur in areas of political and social disagreement were as much a response by the governing élite to specific problems as a desire to protect their ideological stance (at least until the 1860s). Until the challenging forces acquired expertise, leadership and organisational ability, the aristocratic élite could retain control of the established social and political structure to which they were willing to make some changes.

I The Question of 'Toryism' 1815—27

Introduction

The primary aim of this chapter is to examine how historians' views of the period of Tory rule from 1815 to 1827 have changed. This raises questions about the nature of historiography and of the value of the 'generalised concept' in the study of the past. The view of this period that has been generally accepted is that from 1815 until Castlereagh's suicide in August 1822, Liverpool's administration adopted a 'reactionary' attitude towards both political radicalism and economic issues like the Corn Laws; and that from 1822 until early 1827 a more 'liberal' period of rule ensued personified by Peel and Huskisson. This is the view accepted broadly by Derek Beales and W. R. Brock. The distinction historians have made between 'reactionary' and 'liberal' Toryism raises the major problem of definition for the student. What was the nature of Toryism in the early nineteenth century? Is it useful to distinguish between the political attitudes of the Tories and their economic ones?

Liverpool's administration is perhaps most easily remembered for its longevity — lasting from Spenser Perceval's assassination in May 1812 till Liverpool's stroke in February 1827. This contrasts sharply with the instability in politics following Pitt's resignation in 1801 with the succession of five separate administrations in eleven years. In many ways Liverpool's ministry was the logical successor to the Pittite tradition of sound administration.

The main problem facing Liverpool in 1812 was the war with France which had been going on intermittently for nineteen years. From 1812 until victory in 1815 his administration was undoubtedly at its strongest and ministers found a sense of solidarity that had been lacking since 1801. The major weakness which Liverpool faced after 1815 was economic as both Cookson and Boyd Hilton assert. The war had caused some diversion of resources, stimulated some sectors of the economy at the expense of others and the first years of peace were necessarily a time of painful readjustment. It was to be economic issues especially the relationship between agriculture, industry and government which were to dominate developments from 1815. The ministry was attacked by the Radicals for being sectional in motivation as it protected agriculture at the expense of the rest of society. But as Boyd Hilton shows this fails to appreciate the economic policy that lay behind their actions. Until 1819 the ministers, wrongly as it turned out, felt that agriculture not industry provided the better prospect for economic growth. This accounts for their policies. However, this did not convince the Radicals who saw parliamentary reform as one method of creating a new government which would undertake policies for their own benefit. The actions of Liverpool's administration against the Radicals were criticised as dictatorial but they conformed very much with the responses expected from an aristocratic government. Repression and restriction were the methods advocated by politicians for radical and potentially violent and revolutionary demands. This may be seen as the 'political' response of Toryism.

The year 1822 does not mark a dramatic volte-face. The policies and schemes adopted between 1822 and 1827 were already in existence and were merely speeded up. Peel, for example, found that the pattern for reform in criminal law had already been set up by the 1819 committee and the work of Romilly, Mackintosh and Buxton. The reforms that occurred in this period were 'concessionary' and did not attempt to alter the fundamental constitutional structure. These issues are examined from different viewpoints by Cookson and Boyd Hilton.

In many ways the key to understanding the differences in Tory rule between 1815 and 1827 lies in the distinction between the 'political' and 'economic' responses of Toryism. The first essentially conformed to the late eighteenth-century response to demands for radical reform whereas the latter showed that reforms of a non-fundamental nature could be conceded when government thought them expedient.

Further Reading

J. E. Cookson, *Lord Liverpool's Administration 1815–1822*, Scottish Academic Press, 1975

Boyd Hilton, *Corn, Cash, Commerce – The Economic Policies of the Tory Governments 1815–1830*, Oxford, 1977; these two books provide the most up-to-date analysis of the Tories in the 1815 to 1830 period. The following are also useful; an asterisk denotes more advanced reading.

W. R. Brock, *Lord Liverpool and Liberal Toryism 1820 to 1827*, Cambridge, 1941, reprinted 1972

E. Longford, *Wellington: Pillar of State*, Weidenfeld and Nicolson, 1972, second volume of a study of one of the leading participants; very readable

*A. Mitchell, *The Whigs in Opposition 1815–30*, Oxford, 1967, provides a view of the period from a Whig perspective

E. P. Thompson, *The Making of the English Working Class*, 1963, Penguin edn 1968, exasperating and thought provoking study of the development of class; considers the Tory policies 'from below' – essential sixth–form reading

1 A Textbook Viewpoint of Toryism

Fiscal questions were also important after the war. In 1815 Parliament passed a Corn Law prohibiting the importation of foreign corn in Britain. . . . In 1816 the House of Commons revolted against the Government and refused to continue the income tax, first levied in 1798. As a result, tariff rates had to be increased in the Budget of 1819. In that year also it was decided to return to gold currency, abandoned in 1797.

In 1816 there appeared all over the country a network of societies, the Hampden Clubs, appealing to working-men by a low subscription of 1d. a week, and advocating radical Parliamentary reform. . . . A series of meetings culminated at St. Peter's Field, Manchester, on August 16th. The magistrates ordered the yeomanry to arrest the speaker, Henry Hunt. The yeomanry failed, and had to be rescued by regular cavalry. This was the 'Peterloo Massacre'. The Government's reaction was to congratulate the magistrates, to increase the size of the army and to obtain from Parliament 'the Six Acts', the chief provisions of which were a still severer limitation of the right of public meeting and a further restriction of the freedom of the Press . . . .

. . . From about the time when Canning succeeded Castlereagh the Tories became domestic reformers. Early in 1822 Lord Sidmouth had been replaced as Home Secretary by Robert Peel . . . in the following year F. J. Robinson became Chancellor of the Exchequer and William Huskisson President of the Board of Trade. All these men, like Lord Liverpool himself, were moderate Free Traders; and in the next few years, particularly in the Budget of 1825, the Government somewhat reduced tariff rates and greatly simplified the exceedingly complicated tariff system. . . . In 1823 Peel took up the cause [judicial reform] and abolished the death penalty for a further 100 offences. . . . These were the years of 'Liberal Toryism'. . . . 'Liberal Toryism' of the 1820's . . . was the resultant of many forces whose stability was precarious. The preference of the King and the House of Lords, and probably the electorate, were for the Tories as against the Whigs. But the major common ground they shared for this preference was Protestant feeling. The leaders of the Tories were much more liberal than most of their Parliamentary supporters, and also much more aware of public opinion. The King's wishes overtly, and party and public feeling implicitly, kept Catholic emancipation an open question within the Cabinet, though most 'Liberal Tories' supported it, they could not remain Ministers, and so could not carry out other reforms, unless they acquiesced in this situation — until 1829. Moreover the King and the House of Lords were firm against 'fundamental reform'. By comparison with what had gone before, the measures of the Administration between 1822 and 1827 seem notably liberal and reformist. By comparison with what followed they seem merely trivial tinkering. . . . The law could be 'consolidated' but not reformed. Nothing serious could be done about the Church. Slavery could not be abolished. It is significant that it was in foreign policy that liberalism seemed most pronounced. It is significant also that even here there was a greater change of style than of substance. But the respectable public was temporarily satisfied that reform could proceed without constitutional change.

D. Beales, *From Castlereagh to Gladstone 1815—1885*, 1969, pp 22—4, 78—9

Questions

a (i) What was meant by 'tariff rates' (line 5) in the early nineteenth century, and why were they such contentious issues?

(ii) What were 'the Six Acts' (line 15) and what did they attempt to do?

(iii) Explain the meaning of the two sentences 'But the major . . . public opinion' (lines 31—35). How was the 'major common ground' removed between 1827 and 1830?

(iv) What was meant by 'fundamental reform' (line 40)?

b What does Beales see as the dominant features of Toryism in the 1815 to 1822 period?

c How do the policies of the 1822 to 1827 period differ from the earlier period according to Beales?

d In what areas did the Tories not undertake reform in this period and why?

* *e* Discuss Beales' assertion that '"Liberal Toryism" of the 1820's . . . was the resultant of many forces whose stability was precarious' (lines 28—30).

2 Brock on Toryism

. . . The economic condition of England in 1820 was the despair of all clear-thinking men. . . . In the realm of finance the Government considered that it had followed a consistent policy, and the measures taken after 1822 were looked upon as a natural continuation of that
5 policy. The change from Vansittart to Robinson was particularly noticeable because Robinson could talk and Vansittart could not, but it is a fact that Liverpool and Vansittart had already agreed upon a scheme of finance which was to win much praise for Robinson in his first two years as Chancellor. In commercial legislation, on the other hand, there was a
10 complete breakaway from earlier practice: Liverpool's Government began, with all due caution though not without considerable results, that free trade policy which was to be one of the main themes of nineteenth-century history, and the beginnings of free trade legislation in England can be dated definitely to 1820. With respect to the Corn Laws there was
15 an attempt to emend its workings in 1822, but this proved abortive, and it was not until 1826 that a radical change was proposed; then Liverpool undertook a measure which would have gone far to settle the vexed

question by a blend of protection and free trade, but this measure was also
abortive, for Liverpool's seizure wrecked its chances in the House of
20 Lords.

. . . The most striking feature of this period is the virtual abandonment
of the agriculturalists by the Government and its conscious seeking after
commercial support. At times during 1820, 1821 and 1822 it seemed that
a new party — a 'country' party — had been born. It was recruited from
25 all parties but its fighting strength came from the Radicals and the Tory
country gentlemen. The Tories had something in common with
Cobbett, they had nothing in common with Hume; but for a short time
the independent Tories found common cause with Hume and his Radical
phalanx in a demand for tax reductions and retrenchment. The Radicals
30 demanded this on principle as part of their political creed; the
Tories . . . because taxes and administrative extravagance seemed to be
responsible for agricultural distress . . . .

With the changes of 1821–3 Liverpool was able to gather round him a
group of liberal-minded men ready to take whatever opportunities were
35 offered for economic reform. . . . The next two years were of the
greatest importance in the history of economic policy. They saw the
application of the principle of free trade, the consolidation of the Customs
Laws, the repeal and subsequent re-enactment in a modified form of the
Combinations Laws, and the launching of a new colonial policy.

W. R. Brock, *Lord Liverpool and Liberal Toryism 1820 to 1827*,
Cambridge, 1941, pp 172–3, 182–3, 191–2

Questions

a (i) Why was the 'economic condition of England in 1820 . . . the
despair of all clear-thinking men' (lines 1–2)?
(ii) What is meant by 'one of the main themes of nineteenth-century
history' and in what ways was free trade one of them (lines 12–13)?
(iii) What were 'protection and free trade' (line 18) and in what ways
did they represent the old and the new?
(iv) Both Cobbett and Hume were Radicals. Given this, explain
Brock's statement (lines 26–27).
b To what extent does Brock see the 1820–1822 period as a turning-
point in terms of economic policies? How valid do you think his
assertions are?
c Why did Radicals and Tory independent members act together in the
1820–1822 period? Explain how this could occur given their
antagonistic ideological positions.
d How does Brock's view of this period differ from Boyd Hilton's?
* e Is it really possible to talk about 'economic policies' in this period in
any meaningful sense?

3 Cookson on Toryism – a Reinterpretation

The most frequently encountered interpretation of British politics between Waterloo and Canning's return to power is that of a reactionary government under increasing pressure from outside suddenly making good by bringing in men of more liberal inclination. Among historians it
5 was the liberals of a succeeding generation who first wrote in these terms. To Harriet Martineau writing in the 1840's 'the government had no love from any class – very little respect, intense hatred from many – slavish fear from more', and Castlereagh's suicide came 'as a ray of hope in the midst of thickest darkness'. To Spencer Walpole, Eldon was 'the genius
10 which withstood all reform' and 'Londonderry regarded a Radical with the feelings with which a Francis or an Alexander regarded a Carbonaro'. 'Englishmen enjoyed less real liberty than at any time since the Revolution of 1688', until 'the Tory party, under new guidance . . . deserted its old colours' and for 'the first time in its history . . . had
15 the courage to pass over to the popular cause'.

In fact, Liverpool's administration was neither reactionary nor suddenly reformist in 1822. While it did attempt to suppress opinion which it found abhorrent, it acted not so much on behalf of an aristocracy intent on maintaining its privileges as on behalf of a considerable part of
20 society which refused to believe in the political, if not moral, worth of the 'lower sort of people'. An awareness of the importance of 'respectable' opinion not formally represented in the institution of the state characterised every notable transaction of the government. It encouraged its steady pursuit of economical reform and partly explained the interest it
25 acquired in legal reform; it ensured that the inquiry into the currency question would achieve serious results; . . . it both made capitulation to the agriculturalists impossible and gave representations in favour of 'freer' trade their maximum effect. The ministers knew well that the old order's chances of survival were greatly reduced if once the new forces arising in
30 society found little or nothing to admire in it. . . . The charge of 'reaction' levelled against Liverpool and his colleagues is usually based, following the example of the Victorian 'Whig' historians, on their opposition to those popular forces which were triumphant in the immediate future. Indeed they were not 'reactionary' either in the sense
35 of absolutely resisting the 'progressive' or 'modern' elements in society or in the broader sense of attempting to reverse the general pattern of events. They did not depart from the traditional style of aristocratic government in Great Britain in that they were never insensitive to demands issuing from outside the narrow political establishment. They reformed, albeit
40 slowly and cautiously; with some justification at least, they claimed to prefer a 'national' view over the views of interests and classes . . . .

'Improving' and pragmatic as the administration was, it is probably not amiss to argue that the ancien regime was weakened in spite of it rather than because of it. . . . It has been postulated [by E. P. Thompson]
45 that whenever the 'lower sort' became a dangerous presence the

'middling' sort hastened to stand at the aristocracy's shoulder. All that can be deduced from the government's response to what passed between Waterloo and the Queen's trial suggest that this is simplification. Liverpool's administration was never more unpopular, and acutely conscious of it, than when it had to contend with 'clamour'. . . . The fear that aristocratic government would be too provocative and unsympathetic towards the 'inferior sort of people' to guarantee social order was very prominent in 1820. Had popular radicalism not faded away out of sight and, to a lesser extent, out of mind after that date, Liverpool and his colleagues would never have found the favour in the country that they did. . . . What appeared to be a new cordiality towards the public after 1822, most aptly expressed in a surge of reform, completed the recovery of a reputation which had steadily dwindled with the passage of the Corn Laws, the defeat of the property tax and the post-war disturbances. . . . Mainly the Tory governments of the period after Waterloo were held back by their desire to present reforms which would have the widest possible acceptance. They feared above all the division of society into competing classes or interests. . . . The maintenance of social harmony by the state at a time when so much of the old society was being profoundly transformed by agencies other than the state was an exercise full of complication and difficulty. . . . Ideally, reform preserved what was of value and did nothing to disturb the nation's confidence in aristocratic government. The overriding concern of politicians like Lord Liverpool was for the quality of improvement. Belayed by their conservative principles, they proceeded with great caution and great thoroughness, and though their achievements were not spectacular they had a solidarity which was not always present in the great Whig reforms of the 1830's.

> J. E. Cookson, *Lord Liverpool's Administration 1815–1822*, Scottish Academic Press, 1975, pp 395–401

Questions

a   (i) What was a 'Radical' and a 'Carbonaro', and why did Londonderry, Francis and Alexander oppose them (lines 10–11)?

(ii) What was meant by ' "respectable" opinion' (lines 21–2) in the early nineteenth century and why was it becoming essential for successful government to have its support?

(iii) What did ' "Whig" historians' (line 32) believe in and how did this affect the way in which they presented history?

b   How does Cookson explain the early historiography of the 1815 to 1827 period? In what ways can these early views be seen as biased?

c   How does Cookson counter these views?

d   What does Cookson see as the dominant issues facing the Liverpool administration between 1815 and 1822? How can its response to repression be justified?

e   'Quality of improvement' (line 69) was very important to Liverpool.

How far do you think that Cookson has demonstrated this?
* f Cookson's conclusions about the 1815 to 1822 period allow the historian to view the period afresh. Do you agree?
* g The class struggle between 1815 and 1820 failed because it lacked 'respectability' even though it may have had 'clamour'. Discuss.

4   Boyd Hilton on Toryism – a Modern View of Economic Policy

Economic policy was dominated by the need to secure food supplies and stable employment for a rapidly growing population. Ministers supported high protection so long as this appeared to be the best guarantee of subsistence. When the 1814–15 price fall threatened heavy losses on
5 wartime agricultural investment, massive decultivation, and a flight of capital from land, ministers stepped in to prevent an inappropriate diversion of funds to industry, and also to exclude foreign surpluses that were large enough to have ruined farmers, but too slight to feed consumers. They assumed that, thus encouraged, British (and Irish)
10 farmers could feed the nation, but they persevered in warehousing, despite its unpopularity, as a contribution to subsistence that alien governments could neither tax nor withhold. By 1821 intimations that autarky was after all impossible, reinforced as they were by diminishing returns theory, and increasing confidence in Europe's food supply
15 potential, led ministers to advocate a *gradual* resort to free trade in corn . . . .
   This contradicts Fay's opinion [in *Huskisson and His Age*] that Huskisson mainly desired the expansion of industry and commerce, and that cheap foreign food was an incidental by-product. . . . Measures to
20 make exports more competitive, such as lowering tariffs on raw materials, were prompted by the potential need for food imports. Ministers did not expect freer trade in corn to cheapen food appreciably, since with population growth it would increase demand for corn, so neither could they expect it to make exports more competitive; but they
25 did support that food imports would boost sales of goods on the basis of reciprocal trade . . . .
   Official policy was not transformed by free trade ideology. Possibly Canning, with an emotional need to feel avant-garde, and Robinson . . . were more abstract than pragmatic thinkers. But the con-
30 temporary caricature of Huskisson as a Utopian doctrinaire, a 'projector from disposition', was absurdly misplaced. Lacking political though not intellectual confidence, Huskisson was unusually anxious to emphasise his own rigid consistency, while his schematic intellect liked to tie the various fragments of policy into a single coherent explanation. This is
35 misleading, since the main purpose of theory was to justify, not originate measures. Physiocratic doctrine was borrowed to justify the Corn Law, Richardian jargon later to denounce it.

W. R. Brock's structural view that the Tory government abandoned protection as a consequence of switching the basis of its support from the landlords to the representatives of finance, industry and commerce is also suspect. . . . But stable employment was a major aim of policy and ministers came to recognise — especially after Peterloo — the error of their initial assumption that the best opportunities for growth were to be found in the agricultural sector. They turned instead to the towns, as the more likely mass opiate. . . . Even the bulk of the landed interest, after Webb Hall, abandoned dreams of agricultural expansion (coupled with industrial recession) for defence of the status quo, and active hostility to the Corn Laws passed into urban hands.

It is not possible to explain economic policy in this period with reference to material interests and pressure groups. There were, as elsewhere, declining artisans, deluded debtors, and rampant creditors, who gave a terminology to economic debate. But the 'interests' were usually too many and too divided to exercise much influence, so that to describe politics in the period between patronage and parties as those of *interest*, is like supposing that a multiplicity of factions adds up to party politics . . . .

Gladstone once suggested that the Whigs and Reform delayed the repeal of the Corn Laws by a decade, and he is probably correct. Liverpool, Canning, Huskisson, Peel, Robinson, Vansittart, Sidmouth and even Wellington were economically more 'liberal' than Grey, Brougham, Holland, Lauderdale and Russell, though this was less for humanitarian reasons than to allay revolutionary discontent. While both parties wished to appease the lower classes, the Whigs could not afford concessions on economic policy because their only hope of winning office was by economic bribes to the country gentry, who held the balance of power and for the most part regarded the Tories as natural ministers. The Tories, on the other hand, could not make political concessions because their monopoly of landed support depended on their stand against 'Reform'. Liverpool relied on the squires' hatred of political reform in pressing them to accept inimical economic measures that might help to stave off revolution. Peel was to gamble on the same strategy in 1846, but forgot that with 'Reform' out of the way, the Whig bogey could no longer be held *in terrorem* over his backbenchers.

Boyd Hilton, *Corn, Cash, Commerce — The Economic Policies of the Tory Governments 1815—1830*, Oxford, 1977, pp 303—7

Questions

a (i) What is economic policy? In what ways did a 'rapidly growing population' and its effects on 'secure food supplies and stable employment' (lines 1—2) dominate policy?
(ii) Explain 'Physiocratic doctrine' and 'Richardian jargon' and with reference to the Corn Laws, substantiate Boyd Hilton's assertion that

'the main purpose of theory was to justify, not originate measures' (lines 35-37).

(iii) What was meant by 'patronage', 'parties' and 'interest' in the early nineteenth century (lines 54-5)?

(iv) With reference to lines 69-74, explain why Liverpool succeeded and Peel failed to carry their party on the issue of economic reform.

b   What does Boyd Hilton conclude were the most important causes of Tory economic policy in this period?

c   What views of this period have Fay and Brock put forward and how does Boyd Hilton criticise them?

d   Do you think Boyd Hilton is correct in agreeing with the view expressed by Gladstone (lines 57-62)?

* e   How far do you think that Boyd Hilton argues that it is possible to distinguish between 'economic' and 'political' Toryism in this period?

* f   Boyd Hilton argued that by 1822 agriculture had accepted that it was no longer economically pre-eminent. How valid an assertion is this in relation to the 1822 - 1830 period?

Further Work

a   'Liberal Toryism' is an outmoded concept for the historian. It is much better to discuss the 1815 - 1827 period in terms of 'political' and 'economic' Toryism. Do you agree?

b   Which of the leading Tories do you think was most important in the period 1815 - 1827, and why?

c   This section has been primarily concerned with the period from the viewpoint of 'Toryism'. Examine the same period from (i) the Whig and (ii) the Radical positions.

d   In the period between Waterloo and the Queen's trial, demands for parliamentary reform proliferated but in the 1820s these demands were silent. Why?

e   The accepted generalisations about a particular historical subject need to be challenged continually if history is to progress. Discuss.

II The Reform Act of 1832

Introduction

The constitutional changes of 1828–1832, particularly the Reform Act, mark the beginnings of an important alteration in the balance of power in British society. The repeal of the Test and Corporation Acts and Catholic Emancipation broke the spiritual monopoly of Anglicanism. That fundamental change, in 1828 and 1829, made it less justifiable to retain an electoral system based upon principles which, though perhaps acceptable in a pre-industrial society were not in the rapidly mobile environment which was being created by the 'Industrial Revolution'.

Parliamentary reform became *the* dominant issue from 1829–1832. Radical demands for change, the growth of social class as a potential force for social conflict and cohesion, the obvious anomalies within the electoral system and the fear of the ruling élite that it was a question of reform or revolution were the main contemporary reasons for the passing of the third Reform Bill in May 1832. The importance of this Act lay not so much in what it did (it was essentially a conservative measure aimed at enfranchising the 'respectable' members of society and removing flagrant abuses) but in what it did not do. It did not introduce democracy, nor did it aim to. It did not give the 'middle classes' control of the political system which continued to lie with the aristocratic élite until at least 1867. Its achievements lay in creating a political atmosphere in which the question of fundamental reform was acceptable and not considered to be totally revolutionary and within which political ideas, other than those of the aristocratic élite could be integrated.

The primary and secondary materials printed below aim to look at one particular aspect of the reform agitation, the general election of 1830. The documents give three contemporary impressions of this election, from a Whig, Tory and broadly 'middle class' viewpoint, and two accounts by historians, one French and one British. The accession of William IV had important political consequences for the Whigs as the long-standing royal veto on Earl Grey was removed. This meant that either a Whig or a broadly-based Tory government could now be returned. Until 1867 there had to be a General Election within six months of the monarch's death. This small constitutional convention was therefore of major significance in precipitating the whole business of reform. The question of reform became for the first time since the 1780s a matter on which there was real parliamentary support and not just an issue outside that arena.

The results of the general election were controversial as Brougham's pamphlet and the *Reply* show. The question of who won the election does, however, need to be answered. The second issue of importance concerns the effect upon British politics of the July Revolution in France which overthrew the Bourbon monarchy. Did it affect the outcome of the general election or did it merely reinforce an atmosphere of fear of revolution for the governing élite? Halévy and Gash provide two answers to these questions.

The emphasis of this section is intentionally placed upon the parliamentary arena. The selection of the pamphlet as the basic primary document is also intentional as this type of writing was an important way of expressing political opinion and belief. Yet their use does pose problems for the historian.

Further Reading

The following books will be found of value when considering the Reform Act and its effects

M. Brock, *The Great Reform Act*, Hutchinson, 1973, the definitive study of the reform agitation

J. Cannon, *Parliamentary Reform 1640–1832*, Cambridge University Press, 1973, places the question of reform in a longer historical perspective

N. Gash, *Politics in the Age of Peel*, Longman, 1953, second edn, 1976

* N. Gash, *Reaction and Reconstruction in English Politics 1832–52*, Oxford, 1965, deals with some of the major political problems which followed and to a large extent developed from the Reform Act

H. J. Hanham, *The Reformed Electoral System in Great Britain 1832–1914*, Historical Association pamphlet, 1968

W. H. Maehl (ed.), *The Reform Act of 1832*, New York, 1967, provides a useful selection of extracts from various historians

* D. C. Moore, *The Politics of Deference*, Harvester, 1976, a difficult, controversial and yet rewarding study

1   The Whig Attack – Brougham on 1830

The scouts of the Treasury ran about with the story that the general election would add ninety-three (seats). . . . No pains were spared to verify all these predictions of electioneering success. The Treasury were never more active or less scrupulous . . . . The forces of the two great co-
5 operatives, the Bank and the East India Company, with the Weight of the West Indian Body, were brought to bear in favour of the Government. . . . All the other accustomed engines of influence and intimidation were made to play; and the Duke of Wellington, being completely ignorant of electioneering as he is of all the other departments

10   of his new trade, had no doubt he should succeed everywhere, and be able
to stand alone for another session, by force of numbers . . . and in spite of
the notorious and pitiable want of talent which his colleagues nightly
display. . . . did ever Minister yet sustain such signal defeat?

. . . The Treasury calculation is, that, on the balance of accounts, they
15   have gained, in all three Kingdoms twenty-one (seats) . . . . The
Treasury estimate makes their gain forty in England, five in Scotland and
nine in Ireland — in all, fifty-four; their losses twenty-five in England, one
in Scotland and seven in Ireland — in all, thirty-three; being a total gain of
twenty-one upon the balance.

20   [Brougham then analyses the election results and concludes that] it will
be found that the whole amount of their gain is under twenty — we
believe not much above sixteen in England, and only six in Ireland . . . and allowing them in Scotland a gain of four, twenty-six. Now
grant we have underrated their gain by six, this leaves them losers by
25   twenty upon the result as a whole. . . . Let us then observe how the
Government supporters bear their share of the popular representation.
First, as to the counties, — there are in England forty counties, of eighty-
two members which they return, no more than twenty-eight are steady
supporters of the Ministry. . . . Did ever Minister yet meet Parliament
30   with such a preponderance of the county representation against him? Of
the thirteen great popular cities and boroughs with hun-
dreds . . . returning twenty-eight members, only three seats are held by
decided ministerial men . . . there are sixty-two other places which may
have contests — being more or less open — they return one hundred and
35   twenty six members, of these only forty seven are ministerial. . . . The
people of England have begun to exert the power with which extended
knowledge arms countless numbers, and they will, beyond all doubt,
obtain an influence in the management of their own affairs com-
mensurate with their just title to it. They have thoroughly discovered
40   their own Cambridgeshire . . . bear witness to it. Woe to the rest of the
community, if they long remain blind to it, or incredulous of it, or
careless of the consequences which must, and that speedily, flow from it!

[Brougham then goes on to consider Wellington and the 1830
Revolution in France coming to the following conclusions]. First of all, it
45   may teach him that an army is more to be depended upon in the field than
in the city. . . . Last of all, the effects of the French Revolution must
teach him the absolute necessity of reforms in all the abuses of our system.
This is a fruitful topic, and as he is really, to all appearances, not destined
to be the Minister who shall regulate them . . . that if he persists in
50   clinging by the helm he has not the strength to hold, not a debate will take
place in which he . . . will not sorely feel the effects of the French
Revolution.

> *The Result of the General Election; or, what has the Duke of
> Wellington gained by the Dissolution?*, pamphlet attributed to
> Henry Brougham, London, 1830

Questions

a   (i) What were 'influence and intimidation' and why were they viewed by Brougham as 'accustomed engines' (lines 7–8)?

    (ii) What was meant by the 'county representation' (lines 29–30) and why did Brougham see their lack of support as a major flow in Wellington's administration?

    (iii) What effects does Brougham see as the result of 'extended knowledge' and 'countless numbers' (lines 35–39)? Is he advocating a democratic political system?

    (iv) Why do you think that 'an army is more to be depended upon in the field than in the city' (lines 45–6)?

b   How does Brougham's calculation of the strength of Wellington differ from the Treasury calculation?

c   What does Brougham mean by 'the popular representation' (line 26) and why does he place such emphasis upon it?

d   What conclusions does Brougham come to about the 1830 Revolution? How valid do you think his conclusions are?

* e   Who was Henry Brougham and what part did he play in the reform agitation of 1829–32?

* f   The influence of bodies like the Treasury, the Bank and the East India Company, that Brougham mentions, was by no means as great as he implies. How true is this statement?

* g   In talking about numbers Brougham misses the point of the importance of the 1830 election. Do you agree?

2   The Tory Reply

. . . In contradiction to the writer of the pamphlet before us, it appears, on investigation, that there was never a period of general election at which the government interfered less actively than during the late contests . . . and to the assertions that the East India Company, the Bank
5 of England, and the West Indian Body, had combined their influence in favour of the administration . . . the following facts will afford sufficient reply. First, with regard to the East India Company that corporation had not increased its weight in the representation by one single member . . . . The Bank of England has increased its power in the legislature
10 by the magnificent addition of one member . . . . [The writer then goes on to consider Brougham's critique of the losses and gains and concludes that the gain was in Wellington's favour.]

But we are now about to address ourselves to a still more important topic, namely the increased moral influence of the Wellington
15 Administration; and this to us appears the grand key-stone of our reply . . . . This moral influence arises from two sources; first, the political character of the members of the administration; and secondly, the line of policy which they have adopted; . . . incidental to these will

be the character of the opposition to the men, and their
20 measures . . . . The Duke unites firmness, talent and honesty in a degree
hitherto unequalled . . . he combines the rare power of at once deciding
what ought to be done, the manner of its execution, and the mode of its
communication. . . . In the short space of two and a half years the
Ministry of the Duke of Wellington has pacified, under peculiar
25 circumstances one of the most important parts of the United
Empire . . . amended the laws of the land . . . placed the police of the
Metropolis on a new and efficient footing . . . advanced the union of
religion and learning . . . preserved peace . . . and not the least, has it
enforced a system of economy, which once acted upon will advance and
30 promote itself . . . . It has the support of those, who feel that a patriot
King would necessarily choose a patriotic administration; those, more
over, befriend it, who are favourable to economy and retrenchment, as
far as they are consistent with public credit; and finally it has the
friendship and good wishes of all, who, sincerely attached to the
35 constitution of their country, feel, that in the Wellington Administration,
they possess a government equally anxious with themselves to preserve
that constitution unimpaired in Church and State; but prepared to yield
in certain points, and under certain circumstances, when resistance would
endanger the loss of all.

> *A Reply*, pamphlet by a graduate of the University of Ox-
> ford, London, 1830, in which the government's case is put for-
> ward

Questions

a (i) What does the graduate understand by the 'increased moral
influence of the Wellington Administration' (lines 14–16) and in
what ways does this counter Brougham's arguments?
(ii) In lines 23–30 the graduate outlines the achievements of the
Wellington administration. What were they?
(iii) Why would 'a patriot King . . . necessarily choose a patriotic
administration' (lines 30–31)?
(iv) What indication is there in lines 36–39 that the Wellington
administration would have undertaken reforms and of what type?
b How does the graduate answer Brougham's criticism of excessive
interference by the government in the election?
c How does the graduate justify his argument for the increasing 'moral
influence' of the government? How convincing do you think his
arguments are?
d How valid are the conclusions which the graduate comes to about
Wellington's ministry from 1828–1830?
e How does the graduate deal with the question of reform?
* f How good a *Reply* to Brougham's critique do you think the graduate
gives?
* g Who do you think the graduate was?

h Numbers, not 'moral influence', form the key to political success. How true do you think this is of the 1830–1832 period?

3   An Alternative View — the 'Middle Class' Position [1]

. . . The authors of both Pamphlets are party men and they write for party purposes. When the Pamphlets are examined, they amount to little more than the 'stringing of names' and the 'counting of noses'. This sort of disquisition may suit the taste and temper of the men of St. Stephen's
5   chapel. But has it ever occurred to either Pamphleteer, that there is now more of useful information and sound intelligence without than within the walls of either House of Parliament, — that the middle classes of this country sit in judgement upon all public men, — and that the Outs as well as the Ins must stand or fall according to the result of that judgement,
10   although those who form it neither mingle in the contest of Elections, nor sent Representative to Parliament?
. . . We do want a Reform. We require Members who receive more useful information when they are young, and make better use of it when they are old, than the bulk of our present Members do; — we require men
15   who will be unwearied in mastering the details necessary to enable them to understand in what the interests of all classes of the community consist, and who readily comprehend how such interests will be affected by any measure which comes before Parliament. But this is a description of Reform which we shall not obtain by a change in the state of the
20   Representation, or by what is vulgarly called Reform in Parliament.
Dr Paley has observed, that the object of a Representative Government is to enable talent and property to compete for seats; and that with all the objections that may be made to the British system of Representation it may be doubted whether it could be bettered in this
25   respect by any change it could receive. This is so far true. But if a Member is sent to Parliament by the Proprietor or the Proprietary of a Borough, subject to the condition of voting with his or their friends; or if a Member of a popular Election is made to promise that he will vote according to the ill-conceived notions of his Electors, in either case the Member is a mere
30   Deputy, and those who send him are Sinecurists; but a sinecure is bad whether it is held by one or by many. What we want are Members who shall truly represent and promote, and be capable of promoting, by thoroughly understanding and zealously prosecuting the interests of the country at large, and not be slaves to any interest whatever. This is the
35   Reform we require. It may be assisted by proceedings in Parliament, but it will gradually make good its way whether it be so assisted or no; and if left to itself, though slow, it will be the more sure and mild in its operation.

[1]   Extracts 1 and 2 have put forward what may be seen as the 'Whig' and 'Tory' viewpoints. As this extract shows, it would be wrong to assume that they represent the only contemporary opinions.

. . . I have thus given a rapid outline of some of the leading topics
which will come before the new Parliament, for the purpose of showing
our Pamphleteers that the question now is not who is for or against the
Minister? but who is for or against the best interests of the country? The
power of prerogative was succeeded by the influence of patronage. The
efficiency of the latter has passed away. What talent can now attain for
itself in this country is so much beyond any thing in the gift of a Minister
to bestow, that those despise the gift who are most capable of rendering
him service. He must now look to the sound opinion of the thinking part
of the community. He may always rely upon it. It will equally avail him
against the writings of the old Whigs; the defection and bickerings of the
ultra Tories; the arts of demagogues; the ravings of dinner and other
meetings; the combinations and the violence of portions of the people. It
is proof against the sarcasm of the one Pamphleteer, and rejects the
twaddle of the other.

> *The Result of the Pamphlets or What the Duke of Wellington has to
> look to*, Pamphleteer, London, 1830

Questions

a (i) What implications are there in lines 1—2 about the attitudes of the
authors of the two previous documents?
(ii) Who were 'the men of St. Stephen's chapel' (lines 4—5) and how
did they get there?
(iii) What truth was there for the author's belief, stated in lines 6—8?
(iv) What does the author see as the essence of representative
government? In what ways does he criticise the existing system and
what solutions does he provide (use lines 21—35)?
(v) Explain the changes from prerogative to patronage to talent,
examined by the author in lines 42—48?
b What disadvantages does the author see in the 'party' approaches to
the question of reform? What alternative solutions does he provide?
c What type of reform does he advocate and why?
d Why does the author argue that what is in the 'best interests of the
country' (line 42) is more important than party?
* *e* Does the author of this pamphlet provide a better solution to the
question of the 1830 election than Brougham or the graduate?
* *f* Does the author of the pamphlet put forward an alternative view of
political power? How did 1832 help?
* *g* The 'middle classes' not political parties were the real catalysts of the
reform agitation in the early 1830s. Discuss.

4 The Continental Perspective

To be sure the existing Franchise and disintegration of both the
traditional parties did not permit of a regular battle between two groups
of candidates each furnished with a programme identical throughout the

entire Kingdom. The Opposition was composed of very disparate
5　groups, containing as it did Radicals, orthodox Liberals, aristocratic
Whigs, Canningites, and ultra-Tories, and during the past months the
Whigs had by no means shewn uncompromising hostility to Wellington.
Such indeed was the confusion which prevailed during the contest, that
the ministerialists could even claim that they had increased their strength.
10　But reliable calculations showed that, if they gained twenty seats, they
had lost fifty, a loss of thirty seats. Moreover the composition of their
majority, if indeed they possessed one, requires examination. The
Government secured a powerful majority in Ireland, where the disap-
pearance of the forty-shilling free-holders had rendered the influence of
15　the great landowners preponderant, every seat in Scotland, where the
election was a farce, and a considerable number of English pocket
boroughs. But it was significant that of the 236 members returned by
constituencies where the franchise was more or less open only 79 were
supporters of the Government, 16 were neutral, 141 belonged to the
20　Opposition. Further what were the subjects which filled the candidates'
addresses? Until the closing days of July the abolition of slavery and the
necessity of retrenchment. But as soon as the revolution broke out in Paris
the constitutional question took precedence over every other. To be sure
the attack was not as in France directed against the person of the
25　sovereign. George IV was dead and the new king popular; he was
considered with or without justification as a friend of reform. It was the
privileges of the aristocracy which were the subject of attack, the
excessive influence it was in a position to exercise over an unduly
restricted electorate. In every constituency where the elections were more
30　than a form the candidates found themselves obliged to promise more or
less explicitly a reform of the franchise.

> E. Halévy, *History of the English People in the Nineteenth Century*,
> vol 3, *The Triumph of Reform*, London, 1950, pp 3—6

Questions

a　(i) In what ways does Halévy see the 1830 election as abnormal (lines
1—3)?
(ii) What circumstances allowed the government to secure 'a
powerful majority in Ireland' (lines 12—15)?
(iii) What fundamental differences does Halévy see between reform
in France and England, and why (lines 23—29)?

b　What conclusions did Halévy reach about the numerical results of the
1830 election?

c　How did the French Revolution of 1830 change the questions over
which the 1830 election was being fought?

*　d　Why had the traditional parties disintegrated by 1830?

*　e　In what ways is it possible to argue that Halévy saw English political
experiences from a continental viewpoint? What problems does this
create for the historian?

5 The British Response

One of the Tory contentions in the Reform Bill debates was that Grey's
ministry had only come to power because of the artificial excitement
caused by the French Revolution. The strongly conservative Annual
Register in its review of the year argued that as a result of the events in
France 'the general election took place in a period of greater public
excitation, directed towards great changes in the frame of government,
than had occurred since the period of the French Revolution', and added
that in no popular election did any candidate find himself a gainer by
announcing himself as an adherent of the Government. Wellington
himself attributed to that excitement the major responsibility for his
parliamentary defeat in November 1830. 'The administration was beaten
by two events', he wrote at the end of December. 'First, the Roman
Catholic question; next the French Revolution'. But though he admitted
that over Catholic Emancipation 'we estranged our own party', he
thought the ministry would still have been too strong for the Whigs, 'if
the French Revolution had not occurred at the very moment of the
dissolution of Parliament'.

. . . The chronological coincidence was, in fact, rather finer than is
generally realised. On 28 July The Times reported the promulgation of
the Polignac ordinances. On 2 August came the news of rioting in Paris
and republican success; and on 3 August the English newspapers were able
to give detailed accounts of the fighting and announce the formation of
the provisional Government. By that date, most of the English elections
were already over. In many constituencies electoral activity had started in
early July and by the middle of the month candidates were taking the field
all over the country. By 29 July the first elections had started and by 3
August The Times could report the results in over sixty constituencies and
the return of over 120 members. The difference between the timing of
the county and borough elections was not quite as uniform as Halévy
suggested; but general elections in the uncontested English boroughs
were decided in the last two days of July and the first two days of August;
the counties and most of the contested boroughs in the first week or ten
days of August.

. . . The issue, however, is not whether the British reading public took
a marked interest in the revolutionary proceedings in France at this date,
but whether they were prepared to draw analogies between the
contemporary situation in the two countries or to derive inspiration from
abroad for a forward movement at home. Some undoubtedly were; and
it is perhaps symptomatic that the most important of these were drawn
from the extreme wings of English politics — the ultra-radicals and the
ultra-tories.

. . . Certainly there is little indication that the electors consciously
thought of themselves as following in the footsteps of the Paris
revolutionaries. The English public was immensely interested in the July
revolution, but its attitude resembled less the deference of an admiring

disciple than the more characteristic posture of John Bull giving comfortable and mildly patronizing approval to the belated efforts of a less fortunate neighbour. What coloured in retrospect the circumstances in which the general election was fought, was the fact that it was followed
50 by a disturbed autumn, the resignation of Wellington's government early in the new session, and its replacement by a new Ministry courageous enough to bring forward a measure of parliamentary reform that is still a landmark in British political history. But that, in the summer of 1830, was hidden in the future; and it was left to another general election to win
55 the battle of reform.

N. Gash, 'English Reform and the French Revolution in the General Election of 1830' in *Essays Presented to Sir Lewis Namier*, (eds) R. Pares and A. J. P. Taylor, London, 1956, pp 258–88

Questions

a (i) Why 'in no popular election did any candidate find himself a gainer by announcing himself as an adherent of the Government' (lines 8–9)?

(ii) What did Wellington see as the major causes of his defeat in 1830 (lines 11–14) and why?

(iii) What does the historian mean by 'chronological coincidence' (line 18) and why is it important to Gash's argument about the 1830 election?

(iv) What does Gash identity as *the* central issue in the debate over the 1830 election (lines 34–8)? How justifiable do you think his argument is?

(v) How far does Gash's statement in lines 45–8 reflect Britain's attitude to reform abroad in the late eighteenth and early nineteenth centuries?

(vi) Using lines 53–5 as a starting point, what do you see as the significance of the 1830 election? What does Gash see it achieving and not achieving?

b What evidence does Gash provide for supporting Halévy's claims about the effects of the July revolution?

c What chronological arguments does Gash put forward to counter Halévy's thesis?

d How does Gash explain English interest in the 1830 revolution?

* e Halévy has overestimated the continental influence whereas Gash has underestimated it. Discuss.

* f Is 1832 'still a landmark in British political history'?

Further Work

a Although the July revolution may not have affected the results of the general election in 1830 it did reinforce the already existing fear of revolution. How far does this statement provide the key to understanding why reform occurred eventually in 1832?

b   Ideology not personality can alone explain the passage of reform in
     1832. Discuss.
c   How far did radical demands for reform affect the passage of the
     Reform Bill in 1832?
d   How much change in the basic political processes did the Reform Act
     really make?
e   What can the reform agitation of 1829–1832 tell us about the process
     of political change in a rapidly developing society?

III   The New Poor Law

Introduction

For several generations, people's attitudes to the workhouse were not formed by reading Charles Dickens' *Oliver Twist* but by close knowledge of the way of life inside these institutions: it was not uncommon for mothers to threaten their daughters with the 'spike' (as the workhouse mentioned in the documents of this section was called) if they became pregnant before marriage! As it is now nearly fifty years since the abolition of the workhouses the historian is faced with one of his basic problems: how to recreate in his mind the feelings and ideas of people living in conditions very different from his own. The ability to *empathise* is, of course, of value in many facets of everyday life as well as in the study of history.

The documents aim to clothe the bare facts of the 1834 Poor Law Amendment Act. The emotional poem by Fulcher raises questions about the value of this type of evidence; *Oliver Twist* might also be considered in this light.

The documents relating to the Thingoe Union workhouse in Bury St Edmunds, Suffolk, aim also to outline the approach of the Local History Classroom Project (1974–7), in particular the two steps suggested by Beverley Labbett, the project director. The first is an exploration of two questions through the study of historical evidence relating directly to a local community: (i) How far can the *available* evidence be squeezed legitimately to write reliable history? and (ii) What questions are raised but unresolved by the study of the evidence? This leads to the further question, using wider evidence (iii) In what ways can we relate the local, the regional and the national in terms of this workhouse? Your locality might provide another example of this type of approach, and a small research project might be based on study of a workhouse during the nineteenth century.

Those who find lists make dull history might contemplate the quotation from Lucien Febvre, one of France's greatest modern historians: 'Pour faire l'histoire, il faut savoir compter.'

Further Reading

A. Brundage, *The Making of the New Poor Law 1832–39*, Hutchinson, 1978, a recent study of the New Poor Law to 1839, emphasising the role of the landed interest

D. Fraser (ed.), *The New Poor Law in the Nineteenth Century*, Problems in Focus Series, New York, 1976, a collection of articles on the reformed Poor Law in action

N. Gash (ed.), *The Age of Peel*, Arnold, 1968, a valuable and wide-ranging documentary collection, dealing with many aspects of political and social life; see pp 148–52 for the 1834 act

N. Longmate, *The Workhouse*, Temple Smith, 1974, the best introduction to the architecture and way of life of the workhouses

J. D. Marshall, *The Old Poor Law 1795–1834*, Macmillan, 1968, a brief guide to modern research

M. E. Rose, *The English Poor Law 1780–1930*, David and Charles, 1971, a good documentary collection

M. E. Rose, *The Relief of Poverty 1834–1914*, Macmillan, 1972, a useful survey

1   The Essence of Reform

It may be assumed that in. the administration of relief the public is warranted in imposing such conditions on the individual relief as are conducive to the benefit either of the individual himself, or of the country at large, at whose expense he is to be relieved.

5   The first and most essential of all conditions, a principle which we find universally admitted, even by those whose practice is at variance with it, is that his situation on the whole shall not be made really or apparently so eligible as the situation of the independent labourer of the lowest class. Throughout the evidence it is shown that in proportion as the condition

10   of any pauper class is elevated above the condition of independent labourers, the condition of the independent class is depressed; their industry is impaired, their employment becomes unsteady, and its remuneration in wages is diminished. Such persons, therefore, are under the strongest inducements to quit the less eligible class of labourers and

15   enter the more eligible class of paupers. The converse is the effect when the pauper class is placed in its proper position, below the condition of the independent labourer. Every penny bestowed that tends to render the condition of the pauper more eligible than that of the independent labourer, is a bounty on indolence and vice. We have found that as the

20   poor's rates are at present administered, they operate as bounties of this description, to the amount of several millions annually.

> *Reports from Commissioners: Poor Laws*, Vol XXVII, 1834, in S. G. and E. O. A. Checkland, *The Poor Law Report of 1834*, 1974, p 335

Questions

a   How did the phrase 'less eligibility' emerge? What did it mean?
b   Where should the 'pauper class' be placed (line 10)?

   c   What was the implied criticism of the 1795 Speenhamland system?

*   *d*   What criticisms were made of the 1834 act?

*   *e*   To what extent was the New Poor Law after 1834 influenced by the *real* plight of the poor?

2 The Effects of Reform

. . . Thronged was the Board-room on the audience day,
And scarcely could he force his weary way
Through the dense mass, who yet to him were kind; —
'Tis from the poor, the poor their pity find;
5 Oft had they shared with him their scanty meal,
With hearts that kindred woes had taught to feel!

A hectic flush across his features passed
When, long delayed, his turn arrived at last,
And manhood strove, but vainly strove to hide
10 The last sad tears of fast departing pride; —
His was an artless tale — yet kindly heard,
'He had been sick, — expences had incurred
Beyond his little means, and would they give
Some trifling help t' enable him to live
15 In that old cottage where his life begun,
And where he hoped his latest sands would run?
He now felt able to resume his toil,
And would repay them yet a little while.'
— The Guardian for his Parish, kindly prayed
20 That they would grant the Man some little aid;
Told of his industry in time of health,
How honest labour was his only wealth;
Spoke of his worth, which all the village knew,
And what to suffering worth is always due!
25 — A friendly feeling, generous and strong
Spread through the Board — they felt it must be wrong
The slender pittance harshly to refuse,
But they, alas! were left no power to choose;
The Man was able by his work to live,
30 And further aid, it was not their's to give; —
They offer'd him 'The House', 'or they would take
Two of his children, for their Father's sake'.
The poor Man's heart sunk in him as he heard
Their last resolve; each kind consoling word
35 Unheeded fell, he slowly turned aside,
The tear of mental agony to hide,
Back to his bare-walled cottage took his way,
And wept with those he loved, the tedious night away.

Awhile struggled on, all loth to break
40 Their household band, the proffered aid to take;
Doled out their scanty bread with frugal care,
Like famish'd ship-wreck'd Seamen, share by share; —
This could not last; — then came the dreaded day,
When they would send a part at least away;
45 But crowding round, the weeping children hung
Upon his knees, or to his garments clung; —
'Father!' 'dear Father!' 'Oh not me!' 'not me!'
Each wildly shrieked in childish agony;
The youngest clasped her little hands, and prayed
50 She might not go — 'I shall·be so afraid
In the dark night, dear Mother, when I wake,
And you not there your little Jane to take.'
    Her apron-folds close pressed upon her face,
Through which the oozing tears you still might trace,
55 And hear the stifled sobs, her frame that rent;
The Mother on her Husband's shoulder leant,
Till all her weak resolve again gave way,
'She would decide upon some future day
Which should be left, and which be sent away.'
60 Unable still to sever love's strong tie,
They would together live — together die.
Could his exhausted frame have known repose,
His harrassed mind a respite from its woes,
Had but the aid that wasted strength requires,
65 When baffled in the strife disease retires,
Been timely given, perchance he had retrieved
His ruined fortunes and fresh hopes conceived;
The kind physician too, whose open door
Freely received the sick and suff'ring poor,
70 Gave his opinion, that the crisis past,
With rest and care he would recover fast,
But anxious to redeem affliction's hours,
He tasked too soon his yet enfeebled powers . . . .

    G. W. Fulcher, *The Village Paupers and other Poems*, 1845,
    pp 32—5

Questions

a What 'Board-room' is referred to here (line 1)?
b What was 'The House' (line 31)?
c What was the function of the parish guardian?
d How effective is this poem as a comment on the 1834 act?
e E. L. Doctorow wrote, 'We are talking about a belief that there is an
   approximation of truth through the imagination that is not possible

with undue deference to fact.' What is the value of fiction to the historian?

3   A Local Case–Study I

. . . There are in Suffolk twenty large WORKHOUSES, having accommodations for 7,000 paupers; but in summer, they have seldom as many as 3,000, and in winter, rarely more than 5,000 inmates. Eight of the largest are old incorporated '*Houses of Industry*', built in the latter part of the last century, under Gilbert's and local Acts . . . ten large new workhouses have been erected and the old ones have been enlarged or altered, so as to adapt them to the new system. . . . The out-door able bodied paupers were very numerous in all parts of this, and other agricultural counties, owing to the long continued mal-administration of the old poor law, which was eating, like canker, into the heart of the nation, pauperising the labourers, taking away the motive and the reward of industry, and oppressing that capital which should employ and remunerate labour.

William White, *History, Gazeteer, and Directory of Suffolk*, 1844, pp 17—18

THINGOE UNION, formed under the new Poor Law, comprises an area of 133 square miles, or about 82,464 acres of land, divided into 46 parishes, of which 15 are in Thedwestry Hundred, 10 in Blackbourn Hundred, 3 in Risbridge Hundred, and the other 18 form Thingoe Hundred. It had 16,922 inhabitants in 1831, and 19,014 in 1851, living in 3827 houses, besides which it had 97 uninhabited houses, and 16 building, when the census was taken in the latter year. The total average annual expenditure of the 46 parishes for the support of the poor, during the three years preceding the formation of the Union, was £13,538. In 1840, the expenditure was only £9026, but in 1853 it amounted to more than £17,500, including salaries and other expenses. The UNION WORKHOUSE stands within the Borough of Bury St. Edmund's, and is a large brick building, erected in 1835—6, at the cost of about £6000. It has room for 300 paupers, and it had 257 inmates when the census was taken in 1851. From the centre of the building, in which are the governor's apartments and the board-room, radiate nine wings, with airing yards between them. Attached to the house are eight acres of land, of which five acres are cultivated as a vegetable garden, by the inmates. One guardian is elected yearly for each of the 46 parishes. . . . The Board of Guardians meets at the Workhouse every Friday, and the Rev. W. J. S. Casborne, of Pakenham, is the chairman; and the Rev. Richd. Haggitt and Robert Buck, Esq., are the vice-chairmen.

The following enumeration of the parishes of THINGOE UNION is arranged in the order of the three sub-districts, and shows their population in 1851:—

Rougham District.		Fornham District.		Wordwell	56
Bradfield St. Clare	214	Hargrave	489	Culford	348
Bradfield St. George	486	Denham	218	Ingham	233
Rougham	1079	Barrow	1120	Ixworth District.	
Rushbrooke	181	Great Saxham	293	Timworth	241
Little Whelnetham	178	Little Saxham	191	Ampton	131
Bradfield-Combust	203	Ickworth	71	Great Livermere	301
Stanningfield	320	Horningsheath or		Little Livermere	174
Great Whelnetham	552	Horringer	670	Troston	427
Nowton	187	Westley	118	Thorpe-by-Ixworth	136
Hawstead	520	Risby	431	Bardwell	893
Hardwick ex p.	36	Fornham All Saints	358	Stanton All Saints &	
Whepstead	652	Fornham St. Martin	322	St. John Baptist	1082
Brockley	378	Fornham St.		Ixworth	1189
Rede	247	Genevieve	57	Pakenham	1134
Chedburh	343	Hengrave	240	Breat Barton	855
Depden	279	Flempton	247		
Chevington	600	Leckford	216	Total	
		West Stow	315	Population	19,014

William White, *History, Gazeteer, and Directory of Suffolk*, 1855,
pp 459–60

Questions

* a What was Gilbert's Act (line 5)?
  b What were 'outdoor able bodied paupers' (lines 7–8)?
  c What are the suggested faults of the pre-1834 poor law?
  d From the brief description of the Thingoe Union workhouse can you
     suggest why a star-shape was chosen?
* e These two sources are county directories. What kind of information
     do they contain, and how might they be of value to the local
     historian? (Your local library or county record office should have
     copies for your county.)

4   A Local Case-Study II

Thingoe Union Workhouse 1851[1]

Name of Inmate	Relation to Head of Family	Condition	Age Males	Females	Rank Profession or Occupation	Where born		Whether deaf dumb or blind
Dennis Helsdon	Master	Mar	47		Master of Thingoe Union Workhouse	Norfolk	Norwich	
Sarah A Do	Matron	Mar		46	Matron of Workhouse	Norfolk	Norwich	

Name of Inmate	Relation to Head of Family	Condition	Age Males	Age Females	Rank Profession or Occupation	Where born		Whether deaf dumb or blind
Frederick Vince	School-master	Mar	26		Schoolmaster	Middlesex	London	
Caroline Howe	School-mistress	Un		28	Teacher	Suffolk	Benton	
Henry Clarke	Porter	Un	37		Ag Lab	Suffolk	Heigham	
M. A. Bird	Nurse	Un		33	House Maid	Suffolk	Whepstead	
Henry Pollard	Gardener	Un	20		Gardener	Suffolk	Walsham le Willows	
Ciles Miller	Pauper	Un	65		Ag Lab	Suffolk	Stanton	
John Hardy	Do	Wdr	70		Blacksmith	Suffolk	Thetford	
William Pettett	Do	Wdr	61		Ag Lab	Suffolk	Pakenham	
James Feakes	Do	Wdr	59		Gardener	Suffolk	Bardwell	
John Weston	Do	Wdr	61		Ag Lab	Suffolk	Bardwell	
Samuel Mortlock	Do	Un	87		Sawyer	Suffolk	Hargrave	
George Frost	Do	Wdr	65		Soldier	Suffolk	Barrow	
John Murrels	Do	Wdr	60		Harness Maker	Suffolk	Bury	
William Wiseman	Do	Un	61		Shoemaker	Suffolk	Barningham	
Frederick Loddiman	Do	Un	52		Ostler	Suffolk	Bury	
George Fenton	Do	Un	36		Shoemaker	Suffolk	Barrow	Deaf & Dumb
Joseph Gathercole	Do	Wdr	59		Ag Lab	Suffolk	Barningham	
Samuel Norman	Do	Wdr	74		Ag Lab	Suffolk	Cockfield	
Walpole Cracknell	Do	Wdr	57		Ag Lab	Suffolk	Cockfield	
Robert Austin	Do	Wdr	51		Ag Lab	Suffolk	Bradfield St. George	
John Raynham	Do	Wdr	78		Farmer	Suffolk	Brettenham	
Abraham Payne	Do	Wdr	37		Ag Lab	Suffolk	Brockley	
William Ambrose	Do	Un	61		Ag Lab	Suffolk	Brockley	
Samuel Boreham	Do	Un	37		Ag Lab	Suffolk	Lawshall	
Thomas Newman	Do	Un	41		Ag Lab	Suffolk	Bury	
William Carrod	Do	Un	47		Ag Lab	Suffolk	Brockley	
William Boreham	Do	Un	17		Ag Lab	Suffolk	Brockley	
James Cooke	Do	Mar	32		Ag Lab	Suffolk	Whepstead	
Hezekiah Seeley	Do	Un	30		Ag Lab	Suffolk	Brockley	
Thomas Arben	Do	Mar	55		Ag Lab	Suffolk	Chevington	
John Bailey	Do	Wdr	83		Horse Keeper	Suffolk	Brockley	
John Arben	Do	Un	19		Ag Lab	Suffolk	Chevington	
Henry Pawsay	Do	Un	19		Ag Lab	Suffolk	Whepstead	
James Mortlock	Do	Un	44		Sawyer	Suffolk	Chevington	
Samuel Wallis	Do	Mar	31		Ag Lab	Suffolk	Chevington	
James Malt	Do	Mar	43		Ag Lab	Suffolk	Chevington	
John Ashman	Do	Un	71		Ag Lab	Suffolk	Depden	
Robert Austin	Do	Mar	52		Ag Lab	Suffolk	Wickhambrook	
Robert Woollard	Do	Wdr	64		Brickmaker	Suffolk	Wickhambrook	
John Peacock	Do	Wdr	76		Ag Lab	Suffolk	Fornham All Sts	
William Cooke	Do	Un	59		Ag Lab	Suffolk	Fornham All Sts	
Robert Allen	Do	Un	43		Ag Lab	Suffolk	Fornham St. Martin	
John Wade	Do	Un	59		Carpenter	Suffolk	Whepstead	
Isaac Richardson	Do	Wdr	83		Brewer	Suffolk	Bury	
James King	Do	Un	28		Shepherd	Suffolk	Horningsheath	
Henry Canham	Do	Un	31		Ag Lab	Suffolk	Ixworth	
David Plummer	Do	Un	31		Ag Lab	Suffolk	Ixworth	
William Smith	Do	Un	75		Ag Lab	Suffolk	Westley	
Nathaniel Gallant	Do	Wdr	74		Ag Lab	Suffolk	Barton	
John Bellimer	Do	Un	73		Ag Lab	Suffolk	Risby	
James Head	Do	Wdr	46		Ag Lab	Suffolk	Gt. Saxham	

Name of Inmate	Relation to Head of Family	Condition	Age Males	Females	Rank Profession or Occupation	Where born		Whether deaf dumb or blind
Felix Manning	Pauper	Un	24		Servant	Suffolk	Stanton	
Charles Cage	Do	Un	77		Ag Lab	Suffolk	Stowupland	
John Leech	Do	Wdr	67		Shepherd	Suffolk	Timworth	
Charles Turner	Do	Un	52		Tailor	Suffolk	Bury	
George Sheldrake	Do	Wdr	41		Ag Lab	Suffolk	Troston	
William Greengrass	Do	Mar	41		Ag Lab	Suffolk	Trotson	
John Calver	Do	Wdr	69		Ag Lab	Suffolk	Lt. Livermere	
John Lyas	Do	Wdr	69		Carpenter	Suffolk	Lt. Whelnetham	Blind
Robert Banks	Do	Un	37			Suffolk	Whepstead	Idiot
James Bass	Do	Wdr	70		Sawyer	Suffolk	Fornham All Sts	
John Bumpstead	Do	Un	17		Ag Lab	Suffolk	Whepstead	
George Bumpstead	Do	Un	31		Ag Lab	Suffolk	Whepstead	
William Deed	Do	Un	24		Ag Lab	Suffolk	Brockley	
John Kimm	Do	Wdr	84		Soldier	Suffolk	Stanton	
John Hammond	Do	Un	26		Ag Lab	Suffolk	Risby	
Charles Nunn	Do	Mar	40		Ag Lab	Suffolk	Chevington	
Philip Arben	Do	Mar	41		Ag Lab	Suffolk	Cockfield	
George Jaggard	Do	Wdr	50		Ag Lab	Suffolk	Pakenham	
William Payne	Do	Mar	40		Ag Lab	Suffolk	Barrow	
James Talbot	Do	Un	20		Ag Lab	Suffolk	Barrow	
Henry Makings	Do	Un	18		Ag Lab	Suffolk	Stanton	
Sarah Scott	Do	Mar		49	Servant	Suffolk	Barrow	
Harriet Lyes	Do	Un		27	Servant	Suffolk	Barrow	
Harriet Crack	Do	Un		24	Servant	Suffolk	Barton	
Charlotte Chennell	Do	Un		25	Servant	Suffolk	Barton	
Susan Everett	Do	Un		36	Servant	Suffolk	Ackton	
Maria Rose	Do	Un		32	Servant	Suffolk	Cockfield	
Catherine Chinniry	Do	Mar		31	Servant	Suffolk	Bradfield St. George	
Sarah Newman	Do	Un		31	Servant	Suffolk	Brockley	
Susan Boreham	Do	Wid		37	Servant	Suffolk	Brockley	
M. A. Boreham	Do	Un		21	Servant	Suffolk	Brockley	
Frances Cooke	Do	Mar		29	Servant	Suffolk	Lawshall	
Susan Simms	Do	Un		35	Servant	Suffolk	Chevington	
Ellen Everett	Do	Un		21	Servant	Suffolk	Chedburgh	
Keziah Fenton	Do	Un		36	Servant	Suffolk	Hargrave	
Jemina Wallis	Do	Mar		26	Servant	Suffolk	Chedburgh	
Sarah Malt	Do	Mar		40	Servant	Suffolk	Horringer	
Susan Murton	Do	Un		28	Dairymaid	Suffolk	Culford	
Lucy Mucro	Do	Wid		35	Servant	Suffolk	Hartest	
Lucy Ashman	Do	Un		21	Servant	Suffolk	Depden	
Elizabeth Osbourne	Do	Wid		65	Servant	Suffolk	Owsden	
Sarah Murkin	Do	Un		16	Servant	Suffolk	Hargrave	
Elizabeth Murkin	Do	Un		11	Servant	Suffolk	Hargrave	
Ann Spencer	Do	Wid		84	Servant	Suffolk	Artist	
Eliza Jackson	Do	Mar		29	Servant	Suffolk	Cockfield	
Emma Holmes	Do	Un		17	Servant	Suffolk	Hengrave	
Eliza Root	Do	Un		24	Servant	Suffolk	Horringer	
Honor Drew	Do	Wid		87	Servant	Suffolk	Bury	
Lucy Boreham	Do	Wid		36	Servant	Suffolk	Horringer	
Harriet Marsh	Do	Un		26	Servant	Suffolk	Pakenham	
Elizabeth Bridge	Do	Wid		35	Servant	Lincs.		
Ann Hammond	Do	Wid		40	Servant	Suffolk	Timworth	
Elizabeth Watts	Do	Un		44	Servant	Suffolk	Rougham	
Mary Cage	Do	Un		27	Servant	Suffolk	Rougham	
Susan Symonds	Do	Mar		61	Servant	Suffolk	Woolpit	

THE NEW POOR LAW   35

Name of Inmate	Relation to Head of Family	Condition	Age Males	Age Females	Rank Profession or Occupation	Where born		Whether deaf dumb or blind
Mary Head	Pauper	Mar		33	Servant	Suffolk	Mildenhall	
Elizabeth Bray	Do	Un		12		Suffolk	Bury	
Eliza Greengrass	Do	Mar		39	Servant	Suffolk	Livermere	
Thirza Moore	Do	Un		21	Servant	Suffolk	Trotson	
Sarah Chapman	Do	Wid		81	Servant	Suffolk	Bury	
Mary Gill	Do	Wid		80	Servant	Suffolk	Hartest	
Elizabeth Copping	Do	Un		36	Servant	Suffolk	Depden	Idiot
Mary Arben	Do	Mar		30	Servant	Norfolk	Weston	
Susan Arbon	Do	Mar		36	Servant	Suffolk		
Jane Nunn	Do	Mar		37	Servant	Suffolk	Gt. Saxham	
Sarah Martin	Do	Un		33	Servant	Suffolk	Gt. Saxham	
Frederick Arbon	Do	Un	12			Suffolk	Bury	
Seth Arbon	Do	Un	10			Suffolk	Hengrave	
Philip Arbon	Do	Un	11			Suffolk	Barrow	
Lyas Arbon	Do	Un	8			Suffolk	Whepstead	
Abraham Arbon	Do	Un	7			Suffolk	Whepstead	
James Allum	Do	Un	13			Suffolk	Stanton	
Edward Allen	Do	Un	13			Suffolk	Whelnetham	
Joseph Austin	Do	Un	13			Suffolk	Elden	
Henry Boreham	Do	Un	8			Suffolk	Brockley	
Samuel Bridge	Do	Un	13			Lincs.		
David Bridge	Do	Un	11			Lincs.		
Richard Bridge	Do	Un	9			Lincs.		
Walter Bird	Do	Un	8			Suffolk	Bury	
Richard Boreham	Do	Un	10			Suffolk	Horringer	
Charles Cross	Do	Un	9			Suffolk	Ickworth	
Thomas Cross	Do	Un	7			Suffolk	Ickworth	
Charles Durrant	Do	Un	9			Suffolk	Whepstead	
James Cooke	Do	Un	17			Suffolk	Gt. Saxham	
John Cooke	Do	Un	12			Suffolk	Brockley	
Richard Everett	Do	Un	13			Suffolk	Bradfield Combust	
John Fenton	Do	Un	11			Suffolk	Hargrave	
William Fenton	Do	Un	8			Suffolk	Bury	
Chilvers Fenner	Do	Un	12			Essex	Chelmsford	
James Gooch	Do	Un	14			Suffolk	Horringsheath	
William Gooch	Do	Un	10			Suffolk	Bury	
William Greengrass	Do	Un	13			Suffolk	Troston	
Isaac Greengrass	Do	Un	10			Suffolk	Troston	
George Greengrass	Do	Un	8			Suffolk	Troston	
Henry Garner	Do	Un	11			Suffolk	Troston	
Richard Garner	Do	Un	9			Suffolk	Bury	
James Hagreen	Do	Un	9			Suffolk	Fornham All Sts	
Paul Hurrell	Do	Un	17			Suffolk	Ixworth	
Walter Hurrell	Do	Un	13			Suffolk	Ixworth	
Jesse Hurrell	Do	Un	9			Suffolk	Ixworth	
George Hammond	Do	Un	11			Suffolk	Bury	
Lorrie Jaggard	Do	Un	11			Suffolk	Pakenham	
James Jackson	Do	Un	18			Suffolk	Hawstead	
James Jackson	Do	Un	12			Suffolk	Hawstead	
John Jackson	Do	Un	8			Suffolk	Hawstead	
William Long	Do	Un	13			Suffolk	Thurston	
Henry Watt	Do	Un	14			Suffolk	Chevington	
Shadrach Watt	Do	Un	10			Suffolk	Chevington	
Robert Martin	Do	Un	8			Suffolk	Hawstead	
John Nunn	Do	Un	12			Suffolk	Hargrave	

Name of Inmate	Relation to Head of Family	Condition	Age Males	Females	Rank Profession or Occupation	Where born		Whether deaf dumb or blind
ohn Palfrey	Pauper	Un	11			Suffolk	Hengrave	
Walter Ruffels	Do	Un	14			Suffolk	Bardwell	
yndall Ruffels	Do	Un	12			Suffolk	Bury	
David Rose	Do	Un	18			Suffolk	Cockfield	
ohn Stannard	Do	Un	14			Suffolk	Pakenham	
ames Stannard	Do	Un	9			Suffolk	Pakenham	
ohn Woollard	Do	Un	15			Suffolk	Whepstead	
ames Woollard	Do	Un	9			Suffolk	Whepstead	
William Austin	Do	Un	5			Suffolk	Bradfield Combust	
William Arbon	Do	Un	4			Suffolk	Gt. Whelnetham	
Benjamin Bridge	Do	Un	5			Suffolk	Bury	
Frederick Bridge	Do	Un	4			Suffolk	Bury	
ames Chennell	Do	Un	4			Suffolk	Gt. Barton	
ames Head	Do	Un	5			Suffolk	Barrow	
William Watts	Do	Un	2 weeks			Suffolk	Bury	
Charles Rose	Do	Un	1 month			Suffolk	Bury	
George Payne	Do	Un	4			Suffolk	Hartest	
David Ruffels	Do	Un	3			Suffolk	Bury	
ohn Scott	Do	Un	5			Suffolk	Barrow	
ames Crack	Do	Un	2			Suffolk	Bury	
William Bridge	Do	Un	2			Suffolk	Bury	
William Cage	Do	Un	2			Suffolk	Bury	
David Marsh	Do	Un	3			Suffolk	Pakenham	
ames Arbon	Do	Un	1			Suffolk	Gt. Whelnetham	
ames Greengrass	Do	Un	1			Suffolk	Troston	
ames Crack	Do	Un	2			Suffolk	Bury	
William Martin	Do	Un	4			Suffolk	Hawstead	
John Wallis	Do	Un	2			Suffolk	Chedburgh	
Walter Nunn	Do	Un	1			Suffolk·	Chevington	
David Watts	Do	Un	2			Suffolk	Chedburgh	
Robert Arbon	Do	Un	4			Suffolk	Whepstead	
William Cooke	Do	Un	2			Suffolk	Brockley	
Esther Allum	Do	Un		11		Suffolk	Stanton	
Sophia Austin	Do	Un		12		Suffolk	Elden	
Eliza Austin	Do	Un		9		Suffolk	Bradfield Combust	
Jemima Arbon	Do	Un		4		Suffolk	Hengrave	
Lucy Arbon	Do	Un		8		Suffolk	Whepstead	
Susan Arbon	Do	Un		3		Suffolk	Whepstead	
Emily Arbon	Do	Un		7		Suffolk	Whelnetham	
Emma Boreham	Do	Un		5		Suffolk	Horringer	
Elizabeth Boreham	Do	Un		15		Do	Brockley	
Caroline Boreham	Do	Un		10		Suffolk	Brockley	
M. A. Cooke	Do	Un		12		Suffolk	Gt. Saxham	
Jane Cooke	Do	Un		10		Suffolk	Gt. Saxham	
Sarah Cooke	Do	Un		6		Suffolk	Bury	
Susan Cooke	Do	Un		9		Suffolk	Brockley	
Fanny Cooke	Do	Un		6		Suffolk	Brockley	
Rosanna Death	Do	Un		22		Suffolk	Hargrave	
Harriet Everett	Do	Un		9		Suffolk	Bradfield Combust	
M. A. Tanner	Do	Un		12		Suffolk	West Stow	
Agnes Hurrell	Do	Un		11		Suffolk	Ixworth	
Ann Hagreen	Do	Un		11		Suffolk	Fornham All Sts	
Maria Jackson	Do	Un		17		Suffolk	Hawstead	

THE NEW POOR LAW 37

Name of Inmate	Relation to Head of Family	Condition	Age Males	Females	Rank Profession or Occupation	Where born	
Jemima Jackson	Pauper	Un	11			Suffolk	Bury
Susan Jackson	Do	Un	7			Suffolk	Bury
Miriam Jaggard	Do	Un	13			Suffolk	Pakenham
M. A. Knott	Do	Un	12			Suffolk	Bury
Elizabeth Kimm	Do	Un	10			Suffolk	Stanton
Martha Long	Do	Un	13			Suffolk	Gt. Barton
Jane Long	Do	Un	9			Suffolk	Gt. Barton
Eliza Long	Do	Un	6			Suffolk	Gt. Barton
M. A. Long	Do	Un	5			Suffolk	Gt. Barton
Charlotte Lyes	Do	Un	9			Suffolk	Barrow
Hannah Macro	Do	Un	12			Suffolk	Barrow
M. A. Macro	Do	Un	9			Suffolk	Barrow
Rebecca Macro	Do	Un	7			Suffolk	Barrow
Selina Macro	Do	Un	4			Suffolk	Barrow
Lucy Martin	Do	Un	4			Suffolk	Bury
Julia Watt	Do	Un	7			Suffolk	Chedburgh
Caroline Watt	Do	Un	4			Suffolk	Chedburgh
Harriet Nunn	Do	Un	13			Suffolk	Hargrave
M. A. Newman	Do	Un	8			Suffolk	Bury
M. A. Palfrey	Do	Un	13			Suffolk	Bury
Julia Palfrey	Do	Un	7			Suffolk	Hengrave
Caroline Rose	Do	Un	12			Suffolk	Bradfield Combust
Emma Rushbrook	Do	Un	10			Suffolk	Horringer
Charlotte Rushbrook	Do	Un	11			Suffolk	Horringer
Julia Ruffels	Do	Un	5			Suffolk	Bury
Mary Stiff	Do	Un	13			Suffolk	Chedburgh
Harriet Stiff	Do	Un	9			Suffolk	Chedburgh
Susan Scott	Do	Un	10			Suffolk	Barrow
Esther Sheldrake	Do	Un	6			Suffolk	Troston
Harriet Sheldrake	Do	Un	4			Suffolk	Troston
Hannah Lyes	Do	Un	3			Suffolk	Barrow
Jane Root	Do	Un	1			Suffolk	Bury
Ellen Newman	Do	Un	2			Suffolk	Bury
Susan Boreham	Do	Un	1			Suffolk	Brockley
Hannah Jackson	Do	Un	4			Suffolk	Whelnetham Lt.
Maria Head	Do	Un	2			Suffolk	Barrow
Hannah Jackson	Do	Un	1			Suffolk	Bury
Margaret Cooke	Do	Un	5 months			Suffolk	Brockley
Selina Wallis	Do	Un	6 months			Suffolk	Chedburgh
Henry Rede	Do	Un	12			Suffolk	Stanton
Elizabeth Macro	Do	Un	5			Suffolk	Barrow

1851 Census, Thingoe Union Workhouse, Suffolk, Public Record Office.

[1] The two parishes of Bury St Edmunds had their own workhouse in College Street, quite distinct from the Thingoe workhouse in Mill Road.

Questions

a What is meant by 'Do', 'Un', 'Wdr', 'Ag Lab'?

b How could an historian use this evidence? What can *you* do with it in conjunction with the plan, and the population of each parish in the Union in 1851? (The section introduction offers some general guides.)

Key

A	Lackford
B	West Stow
C	Wordwell
D	Culford
E	Ingham
F	Ampton
G	Little Livermere
H	Great Livermere
I	Troston
J	Ixworth Thorpe
K	Ixworth
L	Bardwell
M	Stanton
N	Flempton
O	Hengrave
P	Fornham	(1) St Genevieve (2) All Saints (3) St Martin
Q	Timworth
R	Great Barton
S	Pakenham
T	Risby
U	Barrow
V	Great Saxham
W	Little Saxham
X	Westley
Y	Bury St Edmunds	(1) St James (2) St Mary
Z	Rougham

Key

Aa	Denham
Bb	Hargrave
Cc	Chevington
Dd	Ickworth
Ee	Horringer
Ff	Nowton
Gg	Rushbrooke
Hh	Bradfield St George
Ii	Depden
Jj	Chedburgh
Kk	Whepstead
Ll	Hawstead
Mm	Great Whelnetham
Nn	Little Whelnetham
Oo	Rede
Pp	Brockley
Qq	Stanningfield
Rr	Bradfield Combust
Ss	Bradfield St Clare

——— Boundary between parishes

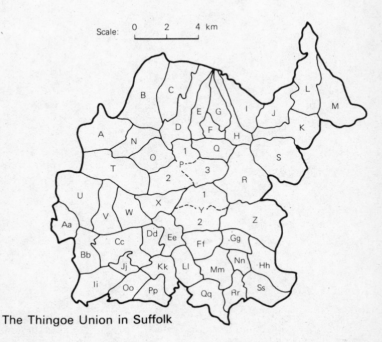

Scale: 0 2 4 km

The Thingoe Union in Suffolk

Plan of the parishes of Thingoe Union drawn by Miss Charlotte Abbey

c What does the census tell us about poverty in the Thingoe Union? What further information would be useful on this? What questions are raised but unresolved by the evidence?

* d Does the Thingoe Union support what is known about the working of the 1834 act nationally?

* e Copies of the 1851 Census for your local workhouse may be on microfilm in the County or City Record Office. Is the picture they give similar to that of the Thingoe Union?

* f How can we judge the reliability of this evidence?

IV Chartism

Introduction

'The Revolution that never was'. Chartism seems to represent one of the wrong turnings of history, apparently collapsing in 1848 without fulfilling its aims. However, from our standpoint, we can see that many of the Chartists' aims – explicit in the Six Points or implicit – were achieved later without violent agitation. Was Chartism then a success or a failure? Who were the Chartists? What kaleidoscope of aspirations lay behind the Six Points? Was the movement based on a myth – that Parliament would undertake radical reform of itself without revolution?

The regional variations of Chartism have been noted; as J. T. Ward wrote, 'working-class radicalism remained a multi-coloured thing in the early railway age, still shaped by local political, economic and social experiences and relationships and by local personalities, rather than by monolithic metropolitan pressures.' The Bolton and Suffolk examples indicate regional differences, but they also reveal similarities. 'Resentment', David Jones wrote, 'is at the heart of early Chartist history.' It was the workers in the old unrevolutionised handicrafts (e.g. handloom weavers), as F.C. Mather reminded us, who supported Chartism more than those engaged in 'modern' large-scale industry.

If the short-term failure of Chartism is conceded then the actions of government in this played as important a part as the local and national crises, rivalries and conflicting ideas within the movement; whether 'moral force' or 'physical force' the Chartists stood no chance against the military, a point made very clear in Europe in 1848 (and perhaps also in 1956 and 1968!). But were the Chartists revolutionary or, as one historian deprecatingly commented, just 'ever fluctuating numbers of men driven desperate by the trade-cycle'?

The further reading list must be consulted for the varieties of Chartism, its active links with other movements, and its course after the 1848 fiasco. Its importance during the 1830s cannot be dismissed – read Disraeli's novel *Sybil* published in 1845 – and the Chartist Joshua Harney wrote in 1852 that 'Chartism itself will survive the wreck of parties and the ruin of politicians. Apparently it has fallen into contempt, and is nearly consigned to oblivion; but in truth its spirit has begun to exercise an influence over the country's politics; and all parties have come to acknowledge the potency of that democratic opinion . . . .'

Further Reading

A. Briggs (ed.), *Chartist Studies*, Macmillan, 1959, a classic regional survey of the movement

D. Jones, *Chartism and the Chartists*, Allen Lane, 1975, the thematic approach to Chartism

F. C. Mather, *Chartism*, Historical Association pamphlet, 1965, perhaps the shortest interpretative guide to Chartism

C. Thorne, *Chartism*, Macmillan, 1966, an illustrated book, suitable as a brief introductory guide

J. T. Ward, *Chartism*, Batsford, 1973, narrative and analysis in good proportion

1   The Movement's Aims

First. – The objects of the Democratic Association are, to avail itself of every opportunity in the progress of society, for practically establishing the principles of Social, Political and Universal Equality.

5   Second. – To this end, they desire to unite the unrepresented of all classes into one bond of fraternity, for the attainment of Universal Suffrage: this Association being convinced that, until the proletarian classes are fully and faithfully represented, justice in legislation will never be rendered unto them.

10   Third. – To obtain, in addition to the extension of the Suffrage to every adult male: that the country be divided, according to the population, into equal electoral districts. That the elections of the Legislative Assembly to be taken annually: the Legislators to receive wages of attendance: and the only qualification required, to be the confidence of the electors . . . .

15   Fourth. – To devise every possible means and to make every exertion to remove those oppressive, odious, and unjust enactments that prevent the free circulation of thought through the medium of an untaxed and honest press.

Fifth. – To procure the total and unqualified repeal of the infamous
20   New Poor Law Act, and a restoration of the spirit of the 43d. of Elizabeth, with such improvements as the circumstances of the country may require.

Six. – To promote the abridgement of the hours of labour in factories and workshops, and the total abolition of infant labour altogether. Even
25   in the present artificial state of society no adult person should be *required* to work more than eight hours per day, especially while so many thousands are without employment at all.

Seven. – To support, as circumstances may determine, by all available means, every rational opposition made by working men against the
30   combination and tyranny of capitalists, wherever the latter shall seek to reduce the wages of labour, extend the hours of toil, or institute proceedings against the labourer, the character of which proceedings in

the estimation of the association shall be deemed vexatious and oppressive.

5   Eight. – To promote public instruction and the diffusion of sound political knowledge.

And finally, the great object, end, and aim, of this association is the destruction of inequality and the establishment of general happiness.

'Objects of the L[ondon] D[emocratic] A[ssociation]' quoted in D. Jones, *Chartism and the Chartists*, 1975, pp 69–70

Questions

a   Explain 'Universal Suffrage' (lines 5–6), 'proletarian classes' (lines 6–7), 'Legislative Assembly' (line 12), '43d. of Elizabeth' (lines 20–21).

b   Which of the Chartists' Six Points are not mentioned?

c   What evidence is there of 'class' being an important issue?

d   What did the London Democratic Association hope that a reformed parliament would do? What benefits would be gained from these reforms?

e   What is meant by 'the present artificial state of society' (line 25)?

* f   'In that the Chartist movement perished whilst . . . [the Six Points were] unattained, it must be judged to have failed' (F. C. Mather). Is this a valid comment on the wider aims of Chartism too?

2   Chartism in Bolton

Saturday August 17 1839

Serious and Alarming Riots in Bolton

In conformity with the orders of the National Convention the 'sacred month' which was reduced by special licence to three days was commenced on Monday last. On Sunday the Chartists marched to
5   church . . . the greater portion having betaken them to other places of more easy and grateful resort. Great apprehension was expressed by the inhabitants of the town that violence would be attempted. At the latter part of last week, therefore, about 1500 special constables were sworn in, and other arrangements made to preserve the peace of the town. It is not
10   for us as reporters, to express our opinion regarding the origin of such meetings, nor do we wish to express our own sentiments regarding the proper persons who should have been made responsible for the consequences. Whether incited by the Mayor or his friends it is not for us to consider, whether the property of the town was placed in jeopardy by
15   the men who had for years fostered the notions entertained by the Chartists it is not for us to determine. . . . The industrious operatives in this town took no share in the disturbances. A number of irritated ill-advised young men were the principal actors. Women with children in their arms, young girls and youths . . . were mingled amongst the
20   insurgents. Mere boys constituted the chief part of the assemblages in many places. . . .

MONDAY— . . . at about five o'clock [a.m.] . . . the Chartists assembled on the New Market-place . . . they were addressed . . . and then paraded through the different streets . . . [at ten o'clock the Chartists
25 were again asked to fall in] march four abreast, and exhibit a second grand moral demonstration. . . . The town was in a state of the greatest alarm; the major part of the shops in the Market-place were closed. To have witnessed the state of public feeling throughout the morning, one would have considered a terrible attack to be at hand. . . . No arms of any kind
30 were displayed by the Chartists, but sufficient was indicated to manifest the animus of the assembly. . . . An immense influx of persons poured into the town about this period. . . . [At this point the magistrates decided to arrest the three leaders]. With a knowledge that warrants were . . . about to be issued the *Chronicle* strongly and earnestly urged
35 the leaders to disperse the meeting. . . . The meeting then broke up. . . . The suddenness of their dismissal surprised [the crowd] . . . ; they . . . exhibited obvious disappointment. . . . At 10 o'clock a dead calm prevailed, not the calm of a peaceful borough, but the boding stillness of a place preparing against an invader. . . . The special
40 constables patrolled the streets, but their services . . . were not demanded.

TUESDAY — . . . at five o'clock [a.m.] the Chartists again assembled . . . numbering . . . about 300. The police officers with the warrant against the leaders . . . made no effort to disperse the mob when first
45 collecting. . . . [Later the leaders, including a Chartist delegate, were arrested and the crowd attempted to rescue them] . . . showers of stones were thrown in all directions, the vociferations were prodigious . . . the commotion . . . arrived at a tremendous pitch. The mayor and magistrates consulted and . . . determined upon reading the riot act. The
50 military, comprising two companies of the 96th Foot . . . was instantly called out, and were promptly on the spot. A troop of the 6th Carribineers, which had that morning been despatched from Manchester arrived in a few minutes to assist the infantry. . . . The appearance of the military as a defensive or if necessary offensive body discouraged the
55 multitude. At eight o'clock . . . information reached the office that disturbances had taken place on Bolton Moor, where a vast concourse of persons had hurried upon the arrest of the leaders . . . .

The Bolton Chronicle, 17 August 1839

Questions

a Explain 'National Convention' (line 2), 'sacred month' (lines 2−3), 'operatives' (line 16), 'animus' (line 31), 'riot act' (line 49).
b What caused the riot? Why was it suppressed so quickly?
c Which aspects of the events in Bolton illustrate 'moral force' and 'physical force' Chartism?
d Is there any evidence that the authorities locally and nationally were

better prepared to deal with demonstrations than twenty years earlier, at the time of 'Peterloo'?

e On the evidence given, why was urban discontent more dangerous than rural agitation?

f The newspaper emphatically proclaims its impartiality: is there any bias in its report of the Chartists' activities?

3 A Soldier's Opinion

[1839] June 29th I hate the poor law, but it is not a cause of the mischief in itself, it is only a train to fire the mine: the evils produced by the manufacturing system and the debt are attributed by the people to the new poor law . . . a population starving one week, earning forty
5 shillings the next. . . .
August 17th Bolton is the only place where shot has been fired, but only three there, and those from the eagerness of the magistrates. . . .
August 19th Everywhere a sudden calm has succeeded the storm; it is unnatural, for the causes of discontent still exist. The fact is that the
10 Chartist leaders' calculations are quite at fault; they have found the difficulty of uniting their people in simultaneous efforts . . . .
August 20th . . . The mayor and corporation of Bolton are said to be Chartists . . . the constables everywhere are, more or less, and all avow that the people are oppressed.
15 August 23rd Men are restless and discontented with poverty in manufacturing places; they have all its sufferings and have not the principal pleasures which make men content under it; that is health, enjoyment of country scenes and various productions of nature. The exhausted unhealthy manufacturer has no such enjoyment; he has no
20 resources but gin, cards, and all kinds of debauchery. The countryman worships God; the manufacturer worships gold: — that gold which alone can relieve him and his sickly family from the misery they endure. . . . Hell may be paved with good intentions, but is assuredly hung with Manchester cottons . . . .
25 December 1st [With the Mayor of Bradford who agrees with] my opinions as to the thrice-accursed new poor law, its bastiles, and its guardians. Lying title! They guard nothing, not even their own carcases . . . they so outrage misery . . .

[1840] February 5th . . . We go on here from bad to worse; the people
30 are starving, and the guardians of the poor are . . . guardians of their own pockets . . . Mr Overseer is absolute despot.

Sir W. Napier, *Life and Opinions of General Sir Charles Napier*, 4 vols, 1857, vol II, pp 51, 73—5, 93—4, 114

Questions

a Explain 'the debt' (line 3), 'constables' (line 13), 'bastiles' (line 26), 'Overseer' (line 31), 'absolute despot' (line 31).
b What does Napier see as the fundamental reasons for the disturbances in 1839? What position did he hold in the north?
c What information does Napier provide on the Chartists in Bolton?
d Is Napier sympathetic to the Chartist cause? What evidence supports or refutes this view?
* e Is there a link between Napier's comments on the poor and O'Connor's National Land Company?
* f Why was the 1834 Poor Law Amendment Act unsuccessful in the north?

4 Chartism in Suffolk

Conditions in Suffolk in the 1830s and 1840s were such as to foster the emergence of the Chartist movement in the county. They were hardly likely, however, to sustain its growth. There were local grievances galore, but the successful assertion of them depended on the mobilisation
5 of agricultural labourers, a difficult section of the community to organise for any period of time. A core of politically minded men in Ipswich itself worked hard in the Chartist cause, but the results they achieved were disappointing . . . .

Many of the more flagrant abuses which had existed before the
10 Reform Act of 1832 continued in municipal and local government. . . . The oligarchical nature of the municipal Government was . . . marked at Bury St. Edmunds, where

> a few individuals, uninvested with any representative character, and uncon-
> trolled by any local responsibility, have become the depository of all municipal
15 > powers and privileges of the borough. This self-elected body appoints the local
> magistrates, manages without publicity the property granted to the in-
> habitants, and exercises all the patronage of the Corporation . . . .

Before the Reform Act, 1832, this self-elected body had the exclusive privilege of electing the two Members of the Borough, and in the exercise
20 of this privilege it generally elected representatives nominated by the families of two local magnates of opposite politics, those of the Duke of Grafton and the Earl of Bristol . . . .

Facts concerning the limited franchise, the existence of bribery and corruption, and the use of patronage were sufficient to excite some
25 Chartist activity. To gain momentum, however, the movement needed the direction of a politically conscious core, and this was to be found in Ipswich. This Ipswich group . . . had been brought into political activity by one or more or several causes. [These] were dissatisfaction with the reforms already achieved . . . , a militant Nonconformist attitude
30 towards the privileges of the establishment, a social consciousness of the

iniquity of the New Poor Law and, to a lesser extent, the influence of trade-union organisation . . . .

. . . the industrial structure of Suffolk was in a state of transition. Ipswich, as the principal town in the county, and a port, reflected in its trade and commerce the needs and demands of the neighbouring country side . . . other industries were developing . . . in particular the manufacture of agricultural implements. This industry was also developing elsewhere, at Leiston and Peasenhall in East Suffolk. It is in these two neighbourhoods, Ipswich and Saxmundham (a town near to Leiston and Peasenhall) that Chartism in the main took root . . . .

Founded originally to meet a local demand, these three firms, Ransome of Ipswich, Garrett of Leiston and Smyth of Peasenhall, had by the middle of the nineteenth century attained a more than local importance in their manufactures and employed several hundred factory workers. In the early 1840s Ransome's felt the pinch. Time and time again unemployed operatives attended day-time meetings arranged by the Chartists, and as late as 1848 a midday meeting was attended by considerable numbers of unemployed operatives from Ransome's.

. . . Conditions did not, however, inspire the agricultural labourers to join the Chartist movement, except in the Saxmundham area. Glyde [Author of *Suffolk in the Nineteenth Century*, published in 1856] expressed the opinion that:

As a body the agricultural labourers have a much keener appetite for bread than for the franchise, and those best able to form an opinion know they are much more anxious to keep out of the Union house, than to have the privilege of entering the Polling Booth.

. . . If the influence of Suffolk Chartism is measured in terms of its contribution to the national movement, its significance was small indeed . . . until 1848 no Suffolk man was ever a delegate to a National Convention . . . .

Taking Suffolk as a typical East Anglian county, the greatest failure of Chartism was its inability to capture the interest and continued allegiance of the agricultural worker . . . the spadework in the rural areas was done by the townsmen of Ipswich.

The Chartist cause in the countryside was hindered by the isolation of the agricultural worker in the social and economic dependency which he then experienced. His horizon was a limited one, hence his resort to incendiarism in 1844 when angered by unemployment and the threat of the Poor Law 'Bastille'. . . .

The periods of Chartist agitation in Suffolk when the opportunity for gaining ground seemed most fruitful were those when the press and the local authorities, as at Ipswich, were sympathetic towards the aims of the movement . . . .

Suffolk Chartism can be likened to a boomerang, hurled from Ipswich in 1838, and returning to its place of origin in 1848 . . . . In Ipswich, by 1850, improvements in trade and in the economic condition of the

worker lessened the immediate need for the reforms which the Charter
advocated. As in other parts of the country, the intelligent workers
80   looked elsewhere for their Utopia.

      H. Fearn, 'Chartism in Suffolk' in A. Briggs (ed.), *Chartist Studies*,
      1959, pp 147—8, 150—1, 153, 171—3

Questions

a   What evidence is there of dissatisfaction with the 1832 Reform Act?
b   Compare the causes of discontent in Suffolk with those of Bolton, and
    of the London Democratic Association.
c   What was the significance of (i) Ipswich and (ii) Leiston and
    Peasenhall in the Chartist cause in Suffolk?
d   Why did Chartism not flourish in the county?
* e   Where did workers look for 'their Utopia' (line 80) after the failure of
    Chartism?
* f   How does your locality fit into the pattern of Chartism, urban or
    rural?

V Peel – A Question of Motivation

Introduction

Sir Robert Peel had a long and distinguished parliamentary career. He was born in 1788 in industrial Lancashire, the son of an enlightened cotton manufacturer. He was prepared for politics by his father and entered parliament as a colleague of Castlereagh and the Pittite coalition. Before he died in 1850 he had come to accept the political rationale behind reform and had in 1846 repealed *the* symbol of aristocratic government, the Corn Laws. From 1812 to 1846 he was successively Irish Secretary (1812–18), Home Secretary (1822–7, 1828–30) and Prime Minister (1834–5, 1841–6). But it is with the question of what motivated Peel to make decisions in the last twenty-five years of his life that this section is concerned.

Views of Peel vary from that of Cobden who regarded him as symbolising his age to Bentinck who saw him as the arch-traitor who betrayed both his religion and his party. The documents printed below attempt to assess this breadth of feeling and try to come to some conclusion as to why Peel created such diverse reactions from his contemporaries.

In the first document Disraeli attacks Peel for his attitude over the Corn Laws. There are certain parallels between his statement that Peel had 'committed political petty larceny' and the belief of Bagehot that Peel was a constitutional statesman with 'the powers of a first-rate man and the creed of a second-rate man'. Both see Peel as a pragmatist, to a certain degree changing his political position to suit the political circumstances. Peel was himself extremely conscious of criticisms of inconsistency, a situation made easier for his critics by his apparent reversals in policy, first in 1828–9 and then in 1845–6. It is difficult to see how far Peel was influenced in his decisions by 'public opinion' or whether he was aware that 'things had to change so that they may remain as they are'. Two aspects of Peel's political acumen are of more importance than any others. Firstly, he saw national necessity, by which he meant stability, as being more essential than strict party lines. Secondly, he viewed nineteenth-century politics through the medium of the eighteenth century. His views were always refracted by this mirror. This point is brought out clearly by G. Kitson Clark. Peel was essentially an administrator not a legislator and in this characteristic he stood at the end of a line stretching from Pitt through Liverpool to himself. His failure, if it can be called such, was not that he changed his mind over fundamental issues of party politics, but that other parliamentarians failed to appreciate that his actions were taken from an extra-party position. Peel's problem was that extra-party decisions were becoming increasingly unacceptable in the political world.

Further Reading

The following works will be found useful for the study of Peel:

G. Kitson Clark, *Peel and the Conservative Party*, Bell, 1929, second edn 1964

G. Kitson Clark, *Peel*, Duckworth, 1936

N. Gash, *Mr Secretary Peel*, Longman, 1961

N. Gash, *Sir Robert Peel*, Longman, 1972

These two works by Norman Gash form the definitive biography on Peel. In 1976 they were conveniently abridged into one volume, though without footnotes. They form an essential starting point for any serious study.

N. Gash (ed.), *The Age of Peel*, Arnold, 1968, a convenient book of documents covering other aspects of Peel's career as well as motive

* R. Stewart, *The Foundation of the Conservative Party 1830–1867*, Longman, 1978, the most up-to-date analysis of the growth of Conservatism and Peel's role in that process

See also the further reading lists of sections II and VI, and in particular:

N. Gash, *Reaction and Reconstruction in English politics 1832–52*, Oxford, 1965

R. Blake, *Disraeli*, Eyre and Spottiswoode, 1966

1 Peel as 'Turncoat' — Disraeli's View

. . . More than a year ago I rose in my place and said that it appeared to me that protection was in about the same state as Protestantism was in 1828. I remember my Friends were very indignant with me for that assertion but they have since been so kind as to observe that instead of
5 being a calumny it was only a prophecy. But I am bound to say . . . I think the Right Hon. Baronet may congratulate himself on his complete success in having entirely deceived his party. . . . The noble Lord [Lord Brooke, MP for Kings Lynn] I suppose, like many others, thought that the right hon. Gentleman was, to use a very favourite phrase on these
10 benches in 1842, 'only making the best bargain' for the party. I want to know what Gentlemen think of their best bargain now? Suddenly, absolute as was the confidence in the right hon. Gentleman, the announcement was made that there was to be another change; that that was to occur under his auspices, which, only a few months before, he had
15 aptly described as a 'social revolution'. . . . And now, Sir, I must say, in vindication of the right hon. Gentleman, that I think great injustice has

been done to him throughout these debates. A perhaps justifiable misconception has universally prevailed. Sir, the right hon. Gentleman has been accused of foregone treachery — of long meditated deception — of a
20 desire unworthy of a great statesman, even if an unprincipled one — of always having intended to abandon the opinions by professing which he rose to power. Sir, I entirely acquit the right hon. Gentleman of any such intention. I do it for this reason: that when I examine the career of this Minister . . . I find that for between thirty and forty years . . . that right
25 hon. Gentleman has traded on the ideas and intelligence of others. His life has been one great appropriation clause. He is a burglar of others' intellect. Search the index of Beatson, from the days of the Conqueror to the termination of the last reign, there is no statesman who has committed political petty larceny on so great a scale. . . After the day that the right
30 hon. Gentleman made his first exposition of his scheme, a gentleman well known in this House . . . met me, and said, 'Well, what do you think of your chief's plan?' Not knowing exactly what to say; but, taking up a phrase which has been much used in the House, I observed, 'Well, I suppose it's a "great and comprehensive" plan.' 'Oh!' he replied, 'we
35 know all about it! It was offered to us! It is not his plan; it's Popkin's plan!' And is England to be governed by 'Popkin's plan'? . . . .

> Disraeli's speech, 15 May 1846, on the final reading of the Corn Law Repeal Bill, in *Hansard*, 3rd. series, lxxxvi

Questions

a   (i) In what ways was 'protection . . . in about the same state as protestantism was in 1828' (lines 2—3)? In what ways was the situation different?
(ii) What does Disraeli mean by a 'social revolution' (line 15)? Was he correct in his assertion?
(iii) What assessment does Disraeli make of Peel's character in lines 24—26?

b   In what ways does Disraeli criticise Peel's personality and political motives in this section of a speech that lasted three hours?

*   c   What evidence is there to substantiate Disraeli's assessment of Peel?

d   How effective do you think Disraeli's speech was as a piece of oratory? What do you think your reaction would have been to it?

*   e   Explain and justify Disraeli's role in the governmental crisis of 1845—6.

*   f   Disraeli's criticism of Peel in 1845—6 was motivated as much by personal ambition as by principle. How far is this assumption correct?

2   Peel as Patriot

. . . I would have given, as I said I would give, every proof of fidelity to

the measures which I introduced at the beginning of this Session. I would
have instantly advised dissolution if dissolution had been necessary to
ensure their passing. I should have thought such an exercise of the
5   Prerogative justifiable – if it had given me a majority on no other
question. If my retention of office, under any circumstances however
adverse, had been necessary or would have been probably conducive to
the success of those measures, I would have retained it. They will,
however, I confidently trust, be the law of the land on Friday
10 next. . . . such a position as mine entails severest sacrifices. The strain on
the mental power is far too severe; I will say nothing of ceremony – of
the extent of private correspondence about mere personal objects – of the
odious powers which patronage confers – but what must be my feelings
when I retire from the House of Commons after eight or nine hours
15 attendance on frequently superfluous or frivolous debates, and feel
conscious that all that time should have been devoted to such tasks
as . . . our political or commercial relations with the great members of
the community of powerful nations?
    You will believe, I say, if you reflect on these things that office and
20 power may be anything but an object of ambition, and that I must be
insane if I could have been induced by anything but a sense of public duty
to undertake what I have undertaken in this Session.
    But the world, the great and small vulgar, is not of this opinion. I am
sorry to say they do not and cannot comprehend the motives which
25 influence the *best* actions of public men. They think that public men
change their course for corrupt motives, and their feeling is so
predominant, that the character of public men is injured, and their
practical authority and influence impaired . . . .
    I should not think myself entitled to exercise this great prerogative, for
30 the sole or the main purpose of deciding a personal question between
myself and inflamed Protectionists – namely, whether I had recently
given good advice and honest advice to the Crown. . . . If you say that I
individually at this moment embody or personify an idea, be it so. Then I
must be very careful that, being the organ and representative of a
35 prevailing and magnificent conception of the public mind, I do not sully
that which I represent by warranting the suspicion even, that I am using
the powers it confers for any personal object . . . .

>   Peel's letter to Richard Cobden, 24 June 1846, in reply to
>   Cobden's letter of 23 June about dissolving parliament, in John
>   Morley, *The life of Richard Cobden*, 1903, pp 397–401

Questions

a   (i) What measures did Peel introduce 'at the beginning of this
Session' (line 2)?
(ii) Explain what Peel means by 'an exercise of the Prerogative' (lines
4–5), 'the odious powers which patronage confers' (line 13) and
'public men' (line 25)? Does he see any relationship between the three?

(iii) What do lines 29—31 tell you about Peel's political motives?
b Explain the circumstances in which Peel found himself in the period between November 1845 and June 1846.
c How does Peel answer Cobden's earnest request for a dissolution?
d Does this letter help you to explain the motives Peel saw as underlying his actions in 1845—6?
e What did Peel do in parliament between the end of his ministry in 1846 and his death in 1850? What would you have done in his place?

3 Peel as Pragmatist — Bagehot's View

A constitutional statesman is in general a man of common opinions and uncommon abilities. The reason is obvious. When we speak of free government, we mean a government in which sovereign power is divided, in which a single decision is not absolute, where argument has an
5 office. The essence of the *gouvernement des advocats* . . . is that you must persuade so many people. The appeal is not to the solitary decision of a single statesman . . . but to the jangled mass of men, with a thousand pursuits, a thousand interests, a thousand various habits. Public opinion, as it is said, rules; and public opinion is the opinion of the common
10 man . . . .

If we wanted to choose an illustration of these remarks out of all the world, it would be Sir Robert Peel. No man has come so near to our definition of a constitutional statesman — the powers of a first-rate man and the creed of a second-rate man. From a certain peculiarity of intellect
15 and fortune, he was never in advance of his times. Of almost all the great measures with which his name is associated, he attained great eminence as an opponent before he attained even greater eminence as their advocate . . . he was not one of the earliest labourers or quickest converts. He did not bear the burden and heat of the day; other men
20 laboured and he entered into their labours. . . . So soon as these same measures, by the progress of time, the striving of understanding, the conversion of receptive minds, became the property of second-class intellects, Sir Robert Peel became possessed of them also. He was converted at the conversion of the average man . . . .

25 He was a great administrator. Civilization requires this. . . . A great administrator is not a man likely to desire to have fixed opinions. His natural bent and tendency is to immediate action. The existing and pressing circumstances of the case fill up his mind. . . . Providence generally bestows on the working and adaptive man a quiet adoptive
30 nature. He receives insensibily the suggestions of others; he hears them with willing ears; he accepts them with placid belief. An acquiescent credulity is a quality of such men's nature; they cannot help being sure that what every one says must be true; the *vox populi* is part of their natural religion . . . .

35 In another respect Sir Robert Peel was a fortunate man. The principal

measures required in his age were 'repeals'. From changing circumstances, the old legislation would no longer suit a changed community;
and there was a clamour, first for the repeal of one important Act, and
then of another. This was suitable to the genius of Peel. He could hardly
40 have created anything. His intellect, admirable in administrative routine,
endlessly fertile in suggestion of detail, was not of the class which creates,
or which readily even believes an absolutely new idea. . . . He could be
convinced that the anti-Catholic laws were wrong, that the currency laws
were wrong, that the commercial laws were wrong; especially he could
45 be convinced that the laissez-faire system was right, and the real thing
was to do nothing; but he was incapable of the larger and higher political construction. A more imaginative genius is necessary to deal
with consequences of new creations, and the structure of an unseen
future.
50   This remark requires one limitation. A great deal of what is called
legislation is really administrative regulation. It does not settle what is to
be done, but how it is to be done; it does not prescribe what our
institutions shall be, but directs in what manner existing institutions shall
work and operate. Of this portion of legislation Sir Robert Peel was an
55 admirable master. Few men have fitted administrative regulations with so
nice an adjustment to a prescribed end. . . . So long as constitutional
statesmanship is what it is now, so long as its function consists in recording
the views of a confused nation, so long as success in it is confined to minds
plastic, changeful, administrative – we must hope for no better man.
60 You have excluded the profound thinker; you must be content with what
you can obtain – the business gentleman.
        W. Bagehot, 'The Character of Sir Robert Peel', 1856, reprinted
        in N. St. John-Stevas (ed.), *Bagehot's Historical Essays*, 1971, pp
        182, 185, 194, 196–7, 211–13

Questions

a (i) What does '*gouvernement des advocats*' (line 5) mean, and what
    are its characteristics?
    (ii) What did Bagehot understand by 'public opinion' (line 9)?
    (iii) With reference to two specific issues in Peel's career, examine
    Bagehot's statement in lines 16–18.
    (iv) Does Bagehot's belief that Peel was 'converted at the conversion
    of the average man' (lines 23–4) show the latter to have been an
    unprincipled individual or a shrewd politician?
    (v) What in lines 50–4 does Bagehot see as the relationship between
    legislation and administration?
b How does Bagehot define a 'constitutional stateman'? How satisfac-
    tory do you find his definition?
c In what ways does Bagehot see Peel as a 'constitutional statesman'?
d Do you think that Bagehot's analysis of Peel's character is a fair one?
    Justify the reasons for your answer.

*   e   Who was Walter Bagehot and why do you think he wrote of Peel in this vein?
*   f   Bagehot's assessment of Peel characterises him as an unprincipled pragmatist. How far do you think he was correct?

4   The Perspective of Time — a Historian's View

He was without question the strongest man in the Ministry. It fed on his determination, it responded to his decisions. There were huge difficulties ahead. The House of Lords was opposed to Emancipation, the Church adamant. Popular feeling in England was largely and the King wholly
5   against it — and George IV was at least trying to be immovable and sincere. . . . Peel responded with the courage that so became him. Retirement would have made matters easier for him and no one would have enjoyed more the chance to return to the bosom of that family for whom he hungered so passionately when his political duties kept him
10   away from them. . . . It was necessary for him to stand on the side of that great bewildered soldier and see the thing through. So he stayed in office and faced the music.
   The abuse was terrible. Peel was branded as a traitor. He resigned from the representation of Oxford University and was not re-elected. The
15   popular indignation even swirled into the small rotten borough of Westbury, from which he brought himself back into Parliament amid unruly scenes in which the patron was injured. The Duke fought a duel with one of his persecutors . . . But it was surrender, not conversion. Peel did not pretend to new light on the problem. If circumstances had
20   been different, and also Peel less masterful, he would have left to others the responsibility for the measure. By passing Emancipation he had hoped to reunite Protestant opinion in the Commons, and to heal the differences between the two Houses of Parliament. He did not think it practicable or desirable to frame the measure so that it would be most
25   likely to conciliate O'Connell and his party. . . . This time Peel had been beaten by Liberalism, not convinced, and Liberalism was about to put forward even more extensive demands.
   . . . In 1832 the King appealed to the Duke to form a Government and pass the Bill to save him from the necessity of creating peers, which the
30   Whigs were forcing upon him with the weapon of resignation. In a gallant and absurd moment the Duke prepared to obey, but Peel wrecked the attempt by refusing to serve. He could not consider it right that men should be responsible for passing a Bill which they had so fiercely fought. . . . He made it clear that he did not intend to act again the part
35   he had played in the Catholic question. . . . Peel's divergence had not been at the expense of his consistency, but in vindication of it. Indeed, it is important to realise that Peel opposed the Reform Bill consistently and conscientiously, since, owing to the general results of Peel's life, it has been considered that Peel's party affinities were a mysteriously prolonged

40 mistake. It is not true. It was in this crisis that the party of defence forged the word 'Conservative' and Peel was a Conservative. He wished to preserve the existing institutions of the country as a security against chaos and the tyranny of mob and military despot, which he had seen follow in the wake of revolution. It was the creed of Burke. . . . He was afraid that

45 the reforms would not satisfy the force they were designed to satisfy, that they would unsettle all habits of obedience, that they would start a sequence of change which would end in the French Revolution being enacted in this country. . . . Therefore, one key to Peel's policy is fear; one description of it resistance, or resistance by timely and guarded

50 concession.

. . . The conservation of the Corn Laws had usurped the central place among the objects of the Conservative party, and a Conservative Prime Minister sacrificing them seemed to be betraying deliberately all that he has pledged to defend.

55 The matter did not appear in that light to Peel. For him the Corn Laws had not obliterated all the ostensible objects of the Conservative party; and, if their retention imperilled the peace and good order of the country, he felt he had a right to abolish them. Nor did he consider that he was in honour pledged to defend them. He held that the words he had used, the

60 pledges he had given, left him perfectly free to act as he thought good. . . . It was a belief which sprang from the old orthodox view of the senatorial function of a statesman and was echoed in the objection which many Conservatives still entertained to men giving specific pledges to constituents.

65 But such a belief was really only practicable in some essentially unrepresentative form of government. It had developed in the oligarchic system of the eighteenth century and survived naturally into the pre-Reform years of Peel's nonage. In 1846 it was really obsolete. If power is to be obtained through other men's free co-operation, and as representing

70 other men's wishes, it must be used in the way they desire it should be used, and have believed it was going to be used. It was not a question of morality, for Peel was acting in good faith. But it was a question of fact. Peel had been brought into office by a party which, however carefully he worded his own declaration, had vehemently protested its desire to

75 retain the Corn Laws. . . . In such circumstances, men were not prepared to allow Peel liberty to stultify his party's wishes and words, and in 1845 his own colleagues had recoiled from his schemes, while in 1846 there were many among the rank and file who were ready to be more organised for opposition and for vengeance. They were ready, that is, to enforce a

80 more modern view of a Prime Minister's position than that entertained by . . . Peel . . . .

The Corn Law crisis must not overshadow the whole of Peel's life, but it is certainly significant. Perhaps the crux of the matter was the change of emphasis in Conservatism which started when the Corn Law controversy

85 replaced the problems raised by the Reform Bill as the centre of politics. Economic Conservatism had encroached upon political Conservatism, a

process of which there is often a danger in Conservative politics. . . . But it was a view that in the end led Peel to reject with contempt that form of association which alone could make possible effective and continuous
90 political action.

 . . . Yet there was a lack of vision [in Peel] for when matters had to be considered in more abstract form — as when he was in opposition — Peel remained too often, and too long, contented with the commonplaces of his party, commonplaces which did not always stand the test of time, or
95 reality, or prepared well for the great activities of his periods of power . . . .

> George Kitson Clark, *Peel*, 1936, pp 62–4, 69–70, 73, 133–5, 137–9

Questions

a   (i) Who was that 'great bewildered soldier' (line 11) and why was he bewildered?

(ii) Why was Peel 'branded as a traitor' (line 13) in 1828–9? With what justification?

(iii) In what ways is G. Kitson Clark correct in his assertion that 'Peel had been beaten by Liberalism, not convinced', and what were the 'even more extensive demands' it was going to make (lines 25–7)?

(iv) Why did the Reform crisis lead to the development of a 'Conservative' party (lines 40–41)? What did it believe in and in what ways was Peel a Conservative?

(v) What does G. Kitson Clark see as Peel's view of the statesman, in lines 61–4?

(vi) In what ways do lines 71–2 and 79–81 show Peel's lack of understanding of the political world that had evolved by the 1840s?

b   How does G. Kitson Clark explain Peel's attitude during (i) the Emancipation crisis (ii) the Reform agitation (iii) the Corn Law crisis?

c   What picture of Peel as a person can be obtained from this extract?

* *d*   In what ways do you think Peel failed to appreciate the changing character of Conservatism?

* *e*   Increasingly political morality replaced political pragmatism as the motive force in British politics in the 1830s and 1840s. How valid do you think this statement is?

* *f*   Peel's failure in 1846 was paradoxically his greatest triumph. Do you agree?

Further Work

Examine critically

a   *either* the idea that Peel as a pragmatic politician did not understand the 'modern' conception of political party;

or the view that the failure of Peel as a politician in 1846 was the result of overestimating the significance of the new social order while underestimating the old.

b   What were the consequences of the Emancipation Bill of 1829 and the repeal of 1846 upon the nascent Conservative party?

c   Peel's seeming 'betrayals' of his party often cloud the historian's appreciation of his achievements. Do you agree?

d   All historical writing is about people, some great and some insignificant. It is therefore a 'social' study. Discuss.

e   How does an understanding of psychology help the historian in his analysis of motive and motivation?

VI   The Transition to Democracy 1846–68

Introduction

The democratic challenge to élitist government in the 1840s had been checked mainly by the flexible character of the aristocratic ruling class. By channelling radical agitation into pressure group activities rather than revolutionary actions the Radicals had achieved certain aims – repeal of the Corn Laws in 1846 and the Ten Hours Act of 1847. Radical movements became less effective after 1846 as divisions appeared both externally and internally. The result of this was a period of apparent political quiescence, what W. L. Burns called the 'age of equipoise', which covered very real, indeed mounting tensions. G. Kitson Clark examines the reasons for this period of retrenchment highlighting the uncertainties of the parliamentary parties and the persistence of 'influence', surely a threat to any process of democratisation.

By the 1860s a different set of political relationships had come into existence which could not long delay the 'transition to democracy'. There emerged in parliament a new set of political leaders, exemplified by Gladstone and Disraeli, sufficiently flexible to see the need for a new social basis for the political establishment. Their roles in the 1867 reform agitation are examined by Morley and Trevelyan respectively, who put forward what may be seen as the 'party' explanation of reform. Both historians mention the importance of extra-parliamentary pressure but see the floor of the Commons as the arena for their élitist views of reform. Liberal historians see 1867 as a Conservative pretence converted into a democratic reality by Gladstone while Tories emphasise the imaginative perception of Disraeli in seeing 'the angel in the marble' – the Conservative working class.

An alternative view of the reform question is provided by F. B. Smith and T. Tholfsen. They see the overcoming of the 'traumatic experience' of the 1840s as crucial with the emergence of a working class movement which was more moderate and 'respectable' in character and yet strong enough to convince parliament that reform was both essential and safe. An element of uncertainty existed and this led to vacillation by both government and middle classes. The Hyde Park Riots were therefore as embarrassing for the reformers as they were psychologically important to the government. This interpretation raises the more general question of when does 'grass roots' reaction impinge upon politics at Westminster and vice versa. There was a real fear, expressed particularly by Robert Lowe and Lord Cranborne (later the Marquess of Salisbury, Prime Minister 1885–6, 1886–92, 1895–1902), that opening the floodgates of democracy would overawe parliament. But as Tholfsen shows, reform in 1867 reflected the cultural triumph of the middle classes. Evolution had replaced revolution as the basis for political change. The ballot box (from 1872) replaced fire and the guillotine as the key to working class aspirations. In many ways the quiescence of the late 1840s and 1850s made reform in 1867 appear a natural step for government to take.

Further Reading

The following books provide a comprehensive view of the 1846–1867 period and the Reform Act of 1867:

R. Blake, *Disraeli*, Eyre and Spottiswoode, 1966, excellent on Disraeli and reform but far more besides

R. Blake, *The Conservative Party from Peel to Churchill*, Eyre and Spottiswoode, 1970

A. Briggs, *Victorian People*, Penguin edn, 1965, a study of the 1850s and 1860s through people like Lowe

W. L. Burns, *The Age of Equipoise*, Allen and Unwin, 1964, places the 1850s in a scholarly perspective; compare with G. Kitson Clark, *The Making of Victorian England*, Methuen, 1965

* M. Cowling, *1867: Disraeli, Gladstone and Revolution*, Cambridge, 1967, *the* modern exponent of the Westminster-oriented view of reform. His views can profitably be compared with the 'grass roots' interpretations by Harrison and Smith.

* R. Harrison, *Before the Socialists*, Routledge and Kegan Paul, 1965, provides a convenient working-class oriented view of reform. A much broader book than its title indicates.

* F. B. Smith, *The Making of the Second Reform Bill*, Cambridge, 1966, perhaps the most impartial and detached book on the subject; compare with Cowling's book.

* R. Stewart, *The Foundation of the Conservative Party 1830–1867*, Longman, 1978, cited in section V

J. Vincent, *The Formation of the British Liberal Party 1857–68*, Constable, 1966

D. G. Wright, *Democracy and Reform 1815–1885*, Longman, 1970, provides a long term perspective on the issues of reform, with documents.

1   Kitson Clark on the 1850s

But . . . it has to be confessed that with 1852 the development of the party had reached an unfortunate phase for after 1852 it is not very easy to read any intelligible meaning into the party system at all.

The Conservative party after 1852 was in reality a survival from an earlier and more violent phase when Parliamentary reform looked as if it might broaden into revolution and the nation was rocked by the struggle over the Corn Laws and the other social and political troubles of the forties. . . . Under the dextrous leadership of Disraeli the Conservative party had in fact abandoned agricultural protection and was to make itself responsible for Parliamentary reform. . . . If party represents organised opinion it would not be very easy to say what specific opinions were uniquely organised in the middle of the century by the Conservative party. . . .

If on the conservative side politics lacked meaning, on the other side they lacked coherent organisation. For more than twenty years after 1846 . . . the Government was normally Whig or Liberal, though its nature was varied from time to time by the intricate personal manoeuvres of a select group of statesmen and a curious *pas de deux* danced by Lord John Russell and Lord Palmerston . . . .

The result was the confused party politics of the fifties. If it is the function of parties to give force and meaning to Parliamentary government, then this party system was a failure; if it is the function of a party system to represent accurately the realities of national life, it largely failed in that also. The forces which were remodelling Britain had not yet forced an effective entry. . . . The control was in hands which had not won it, but received it by prescription and inheritance. . . . As Bagehot complained, Parliament had 'an undue bias towards the sentiments and views of the landed interest'. The landed gentry, so he noted, not only claimed to monopolize the representation of the counties, they also sat for the boroughs as well, and they filled the Cabinet. . . . It was in fact the old governing class of the country, still in control twenty-seven years after the Reform Bill.

One of the reasons for this survival was of course the deficiency of that Act, not only the inequitable distribution of seats but also the limitations of the franchise and the ways in which it could be manipulated. But another reason was the fact that within the framework of the nineteenth-century party politics and under the skin of nineteenth-century life many eighteenth-century practices and relationships were still effective . . . .

The conception of 'influence' which pervaded mid-nineteenth-century politics in Britain had a very long history. . . . It might be the power exercised by the local magnate, very often a peer, over his neighbours. . . . Or it might be the power of an employer to influence the votes of his men, or a town landlord those who lived in his houses. But the best known form of influence was that of the rural landlord over the votes of his farming tenants . . . .

What is undoubtedly true is that influence was a dominant reality in mid-nineteenth-century politics particularly in the counties . . . .

G. Kitson Clark, *The Making of Victorian England*, Methuen, 1965, pp 208–13

Questions

a   (i) How does Kitson Clark define 'party' (lines 10–13)?
(ii) Examine the political choreography of Palmerston and Russell in the 1850s (lines 17–9).
(iii) In what ways was political control held by 'prescription and inheritance' (line 26)? How had this changed by the end of the century?
(iv) What does Kitson Clark mean by 'influence' (line 39)?

b   Why does G. Kitson Clark see the problem of direction as being the key to the 'confused party politics of the fifties' (line 20)?

c   What does G. Kitson Clark see as the function of parties? Is this definition adequate and how does it help to explain mid-Victorian politics?

d   What do you understand by 'influence' and why was it important in this period?

*   e   G. Kitson Clark places some emphasis on the writings of Bagehot in his work. Who was Bagehot and what ideas did he have about politics in the mid-1860s?

*   f   Social class and social deference were seen as contradictory concepts in the mid-nineteenth century. The reason for this lies in the environment associated with each of them, respectively urban and rural. How valid an assertion do you think this is?

*   g   G. Kitson Clark sees the persistence of 'many eighteenth-century or near eighteenth-century practices and relationships' as of major importance. How does he maintain this and how important do you think they were?

2 Gladstone as 'eminence gris' in 1867

The process effecting this wide extension of political power to immense classes hitherto without it, was in every respect extraordinary. The great reform was carried by a parliament elected to support Lord Palmerston, and Lord Palmerston detested reform. It was carried by a government in a
5   decided minority. It was carried by a minister and by a leader of the opposition, neither of whom was at the time in the full confidence of his party. Finally, it was carried by a House of Commons that the year before had, in effect, rejected a measure for the admission of only 400,000 new voters, while the measure to which it now assented added almost a
10   million voters to the electorate. . . . The secret of the strange reversal in 1867 of all that had been said, attempted, and done in 1866, would seem to be that the tide of public opinion had suddenly swelled to flood. The same timidity that made the ruling classes dread reform, had the compensation that very little in the way of popular demonstration was
15   quite enough to frighten them into accepting it. . . . Riots in Hyde Park, street processions measured by the mile in the great cities from London up to Glasgow, open-air meetings attended by a hundred . . . fifty thousand

people at Birmingham . . . showed that even though the workmen
might not be anxious to demand the franchise, yet they would not stand
20 its refusal. In the autumn of 1866 Mr Bright led a splendid campaign in a
series of speeches in England, Scotland and Ireland, marked by every kind
of power. It is worthy of remark that not one of the main changes of that
age was carried in parliament without severe agitation out of doors.
Catholic emancipation was won by O'Connell; the reform act of 1832 by
25 the political unions; free trade by the league against the corn laws.
Household suffrage followed the same rule.

. . . Mr Disraeli began by preparing a series of resolutions − platitudes
with little relationship to realities. ., . Under pressure from Mr
Gladstone the government explained their plan, dropped the resolutions
30 and brought in a bill (March 18). Men were to have votes who had
university degrees, or were members of learned professions, or had thirty
pounds in a savings bank, or fifty pounds in the funds, or paid a pound in
direct taxes; but the fighting point was that every householder who paid
rates should have a vote. . . . To comfort his party for giving so wide a
35 suffrage, the minister provided checks by conferring a double vote on
certain classes of citizens, and imposing strict terms as to residence. Mr
Gladstone flew down upon the plan with energy, as a measure of illusory
concessions, and securities still more illusory. . . . A meeting of 278
liberals was held at his house, and he addressed them for nearly an hour
40 concurring not over-willingly in the conclusion that they should not
resist the second reading.

. . . Lord Cranborne, the chief conservative seceder, described the bill
in its final shape, after undergoing countless transformations, as the result
of the adoption of the principles of Bright at the dictation of Gladstone. It
45 was at Mr Gladstone's demand that lodgers were invested with votes; that
the dual vote, voting papers, educational franchise, savings-bank franchise, all disappeared; that the distribution of seats was extended after into an
operation of enormously larger scale . . . .

John Morley, *The Life of William Ewart Gladstone*, 1908, vol I, pp
643−50

Questions

a (i) Who were the 'minister' and 'leader of the opposition' referred to
in lines 5−6? In what ways did they both lack the full confidence of
their parties? Why did the House of Commons change its mind
within a year (lines 7−10)?
(ii) How far is it true to argue that no 'main change of that age was
carried in parliament without severe agitation out of doors' (lines 22−
3)?
In what ways was this to be the pattern for major political
developments from 1870?
(iii) What does Morley identify as the 'fighting points' (lines 33−4)?
Why should this have been the case?

b   Why does Morley maintain that 'Lord Palmerston detested reform'?

c   How important was popular protest in leading to reform in 1867 according to Morley? Do you agree?

d   What role does Morley attribute to Gladstone in the debates over reform?

e   Parliamentary reform in 1867 was seen by Morley as being a result of Gladstone's parliamentary presence. How far do you think this is a correct view of Gladstone's role?

* *f*   Who was John Morley? How reliable do you think his *Life of Gladstone* is as a piece of scholarship for the modern historian?

* *g*   Morley argues that 'not one of the main changes of that age was carried in parliament without severe agitation out of doors' (lines 22–23). Examine this statement in relation to the period 1825–1870.

3   Disraeli sees 'the angel in the marble'

The working-men, at first indifferent to the fate of a Bill which only proposed to enfranchise a small fraction of their number, were stung to fury by the character of Lowe's opposition to it, and a great franchise agitation, led by John Bright, soon aroused feelings which could never
5   have been satisfied by so half-hearted a measure as the Bill of 1866. . . . A combination of the Conservatives with forty Whigs from 'the Cave' defeated the Bill in Committee, and the Russell Ministry resigned.

The cause of working-class franchisement gained in the end by this apparent disaster . . . the incoming Conservative government of Lord
10   Derby, with Disraeli for its moving spirit, had now to deal with a situation of the utmost gravity of their own making. . . . If the party would abandon its former convictions, stultify the vote by which it had just gained office, and throw over Robert Lowe, and if Disraeli would pass 'the doctrine of Tom Paine' into law, a signal service could be
15   rendered to the Empire such as Peel had rendered over Catholic Emancipation and the Corn Laws.

The Conservative party was well disciplined. The decision would be that of its chiefs, and their counsels were dominated by the transcendent abilities of a man singularly open-minded both as to the main political
20   chance and as to the best interests of the community. Disraeli, looking with a foreigner's eyes on England, often saw things that were not the most evident to the natives. He had put together in youth a collection of political ideas, known to the public through the characteristic medium of his novels. These ideas were, like himself, a mixture of extravagance and
25   penetration, of sentimentality and realism. He specially delighted in combinations which seemed paradoxes to that age; he believed in the Jews and in the Church of England; in the political influence of the Crown; in the 'territorial aristocracy', that is, in the Tory part of it; and finally, giving the middle classes a skip, he believed in the working-
30   men . . . .

Yet even Disraeli would not have ventured to 'dish the Whigs' and to take the famous 'leap in the dark' of working-class enfranchisement but for the agitation in the country over which Bright presided in the autumn of 1866. . . . It was different from Chartism, because it was based on class

35 union instead of class division. The middle and working classes, the one under-represented, the other scarcely represented at all, had come together to demand the franchise . . . .

Disraeli had many years before told the world that industrialism had created a new 'nation' cut off from contact with the governing class. At

40 length he was convinced that it could no longer with safety be left outside the Parliamentary system. . . . Such a country, Disraeli perceived, could no longer be governed by the 'territorial aristocracy' on whom he had once pinned his faith, and, since he had never shared the Whig idealisation of the middle class, he was reduced to admit the political claims of the

45 artisan . . . .

When the Bill left Committee it was to all intents and purposes household franchise for the boroughs. Being sent up to the Lords by a Conservative government, it passed at once into law. Lord Cranborne . . . in vain denounced the betrayal. There was no one

50 capable of playing the young Disraeli to the old Disraeli's Peel. The upshot of these . . . confused Parliamentary operations of which no one of the statesmen concerned had quite foreseen the issue, was that the governing classes had recognised the needs of the new era with a wise alacrity, when once they were brought up against the facts, while the

55 rising democracy had asserted its claims with singular dignity and good sense . . . .

> G. M. Trevelyan, *British History in the Nineteenth Century and after, 1782–1919*, Penguin edn, 1965, pp 335–8

Questions

a (i) Explain the reference to 'the Cave' in lines 5–7.
(ii) What was the 'doctrine of Tom Paine' (line 14)? In what ways was 1867 a triumph for Paine's ideas?
(iii) How does Trevelyan assess Disraeli's political attitude in lines 20–22 and 25–30? Does this help to explain his subsequent policies in the 1870s?

b Disraeli approached the question of reform from a pragmatic viewpoint. Does Trevelyan accept this view?

c Where does Trevelyan see Disraeli getting his political ideas from? How important were they to the question of reform?

d How does Trevelyan explain the paradox of an élitist Conservative party accepting a 'transition to democracy'?

* e Who was G. M. Trevelyan? How far do you think his own views on history influenced his interpretation of the agitation of 1867?

f Disraeli attacked the roots of Conservatism in 1867 just as much as

Peel did in 1846. Why did Disraeli survive to become Prime Minister twice?

g   Why and how were the Conservatives, a minority government, able to pass reform in 1867?

4   Pressure From Without

The cholera and the Riots were ominously reminiscent of the visitations which had accompanied the Great Reform Bill. The cholera carried off 8,000 people in London alone and it deepened the horror of the economic distress in the East End. The Hyde Park Riots seemed to portend a return
5   to the violence of 1831, and although they did not precipitate the cabinet into preparing a Reform Bill they did disturb its hibernation.

The Hyde Park Riots have come to have a fortuitous notoriety, partly because they appear in retrospect to have been instrumental in persuading the Government that the introduction of a Reform Bill was urgent, and
10   partly because Matthew Arnold made them symbolic of disorder in *Culture and Anarchy*, but in themselves the Riots were comparatively unimportant. . . . The Riots of 1866 were much less violent than the Nottingham election affray of 1865, or the 'Murphy Riots' which broke out in Birmingham, Ashton-under-Lyne and Manchester in 1867 and
15   1868. The disturbances in Hyde Park were unique in a mass agitation which maintained an unprecedented degree of order and made their mark because they were a reversion to the kind of popular violence which men could recall from the thirties and forties. Although, as Matthew Arnold perceived, the Riots were incidental to the clash between the
20   Reform League and the Government, they served to emphasize the victory of the artisans over traditional authority. And this in its turn changed the attitudes of members, from regarding Reform as an abstract question for debate to accepting it as an issue which needed settlement.

The Reform League was one of the principal successors to a long line of
25   ephemeral societies which had striven for electoral reform . . . since the collapse of the Chartist movement and the disbanding of the Anti-Corn Law League. The societies inherited the sectional differences of the older organizations and their activities had been continually vitiated by disagreement about their objectives. Some sections adhered to the
30   Chartist demands for the ballot, 'manhood suffrage' and the abolition of property qualifications for members, while others deriving from the Anti-Corn Law League stopped at 'household suffrage'. . . . The Riots gained their vehemence not from the positive support for the aims of the League, but from anger at the social exclusion implied in the Govern-
35   ment's prohibition which ran counter to the general inclusionist enthusiasm of the age. The *English* workman denounced Walpole's order as showing a lack of faith in the good intentions of the working-men. . . . The Riots were a protest against class isolation, not a symptom of class war . . . .

40   This demonstration of working-class independence, and the assertion
of the right to enjoy public amenities and political discussion equally with
the upper classes, greatly disturbed Arnold and Carlyle. They saw it as the
signal of the final break in the chain of deference which had enabled
English society to progress peaceably. . . . The working classes had
45 shown themselves prone to anarchy, and the upper classes had revealed
themselves as having lost the will to rule. But Arnold misjudged the
Riots as much as Marx. The actual disturbances and the League's isolation
from the mob presages the Reformers' failure to convert the votes of the
mob into a viable electoral power and of the mob's failure to translate its
50 aspirations into effective parliamentary action.
        F. B. Smith, *The Making of the Second Reform Bill*, Melbourne
        University Press, 1966, pp 125–32

Questions

a   (i) Who was Matthew Arnold and what did his book *Culture and
     Anarchy* say about society in the 1860s (lines 10–11)?
     (ii) What does F. B. Smith mean by 'artisans' and 'traditional
     authority' in line 21? In what ways did the Hyde Park Riots symbolise
     the victory of the former over the latter?
     (iii) What was the League and what were its aims (lines 24–7)?
     (iv) Why does F. B. Smith see the Riots as possessing a vehemence of
     an intensity uncommon even for the nineteenth century?
b   How important does Smith see the Hyde Park Riots in the passage of
     reform in 1867?
c   The question of 'respectability' was a key issue in the enfranchisement
     of the urban working class. How far did the Hyde Park Riots
     heighten this issue?
*   d   Assess the role of the Reform League in the achievement of reform in
     1867?
*   e   Smith uses Matthew Arnold as a source of evidence in his analysis of
     the Hyde Park Riots. What did Arnold believe they signified and was
     he correct?
*   f   'The Riots were a protest against the class isolation, not a symptom of
     class war' (lines 38–9). Discuss.

5   1867 as a Middle Class Triumph

Although the agitation for an extension of the franchise was relatively
dormant during the 1850s, the issue was still of fundamental importance.
In the new culture that had emerged out of the social and ideological
conflict of the Chartist era, this remained a great unresolved question. For
5 working class radicalism the franchise issue could not be postponed
indefinitely, since it continued to be a primary symbol of the demand for
equality, justice and respect. It was the parliamentary reform agitation of

the 1860s that settled the question in the towns before the legislation of
1867. It was settled in a way that reflected the culture as a whole – on the
basis of a broad consensus, but in the context of class conflict that had been
muted somewhat. For working class radicalism it represented both a
triumph and a defeat. On the one hand the parliamentary reform
movement embodied a forceful reaffirmation of radical principles and
values, which were now supported by middle-class liberalism. On the
other hand, however, those values had been established only in the
somewhat attenuated form so characteristic of the culture, that is within
the limits imposed by the structure of power and status. In parliamentary
reform, as in so many other areas, old principles and ideas underwent
subtle changes in a new context.

When the franchise once again became a live issue for working class
radicalism in the 1860s, it was in a political and social context that had
changed considerably since the 1830s. For one thing, the middle-class
radicals had taken up the issue with some enthusiasm. . . . They expected
something much less than manhood suffrage; this meant giving up a great
deal both symbolically and in substance. For another, the middle-class
movement, coming from above, was cast in terms that made all too
visible the new forms of subordination and deference that had been
developing in the cities. There was more than a hint of paternalism, and
even condescension . . . .

The approach to parliamentary reform that working class radicals
instinctively rejected . . . only to be caught up in its implications in the
course of the agitation – was a standard middle-class version of consensus
values . . . the radicals found themselves arguing that reform would
contribute to stability and public order. . . . Intent on refuting the
arguments of their opponents, the radicals ended up making their case in
the most respectable mid-Victorian terms. By 1867 even Ernest Jones was
depicting parliamentary reform as a 'conservative' measure conducive to
stability . . . .

Nowhere, however, could working men escape the limitations
imposed by the social and political pre-eminence of the middle classes.
The social and ideological patterns manifested in the parliamentary
reform agitation necessarily reflected a culture characterised by middle-
class hegemony. The Reform Act of 1867 fell far short not only of the
aspirations of Chartism but also of its programme.

T. Tholfsen, *Working Class Radicalism in mid-Victorian England*,
1976, pp 315–25

Questions

a (i) Why did the franchise issue continue to be 'a primary symbol of
the demand for equality, justice and respect' (lines 6–7)? In what
ways did 1867 resolve this issue and what questions were left
unanswered by it?

(ii) In what ways do you think 'old principles and ideas underwent subtle charges in a new context' (lines 17−9)? What was the 'new context' to which Tholfsen refers?

(iii) What does Tholfsen see as the characteristics of the middle class movement that evolved in the 1860s (lines 22−29)? In what ways did this result in 1867 being essentially a conservative reform measure?

(iv) What did Chartism wish to achieve and how far did 1867 'fall far short' of this (lines 43−4)?

b Why, according to Tholfsen, could the extension of the franchise not be postponed indefinitely? How valid do you think his answer is?

c How far does Tholfsen argue that reform in 1867 was limited by the position of the middle classes? Do you agree?

d Tholfsen sees ideology and culture as the keys to understanding reform in 1867. How far do you think he has substantiated his case?

* e Reform in 1867 'represented both a triumph and a defeat' for the working class. Discuss.

* f Reform in 1867 was aimed more at maintaining stability than any substantial reform of the franchise. How far is this true?

Further Work

a The accepted views of reform in 1867 have essentially been party ones. How far can this belief still be maintained and has it prevented a real appreciation of why reform occurred?

b 1867 marks a 'transition' between an élitist view of government and a democratic one. Discuss.

c Contrast Disraeli's and Gladstone's views of parliamentary reform.

d The failure of governments in the 1846−1867 period was essentially the failure of party to give direction. Is this true?

e Despite the failure of party politics in the 1846−1865 period it was one of fundamental importance in the change from an eighteenth-century view of the role of the state to a nineteenth-century one. Discuss.

f The 1850s and 1860s were dominated by a series of seemingly irreconcilable paradoxes. How were they resolved?

VII Foreign Policy 1812—65

Introduction

Foreign policy in the period 1812 to 1865 is seen by historians as being dominated by the trinity of Castlereagh, Canning and Palmerston. This is to some degree true but there were other less colourful, though by no means less capable, Foreign Secretaries – Dudley, Aberdeen, Wellington, Granville, Russell, Derby, Clarendon – who played crucial roles in the extension of foreign affairs.

To view foreign policy through personality alone is to misplace one's emphasis. Foreign policy and domestic policy were extremely closely connected. This Castlereagh made clear in his 1820 State Paper and of this Palmerston was fully aware throughout his career at the Foreign Office. Public opinion, that most irrational of all human characteristics, could be roused by the action or inaction of the Foreign Secretary.

Yet, as the documents below attempt to illustrate, there was a certain continuity of ideas underlying foreign policy during this period. From Castlereagh to Palmerston emphasis was placed upon non-intervention and the dignity of Britain, two highly incompatible ideas, and the belief in the balance of powers. The ways in which these objectives were approached may have differed but the principles remained, constantly being reiterated in parliament.

Castlereagh became Foreign Secretary in 1812. Britain had been at war with Revolutionary and Napoleonic France for nearly twenty years. Britain's involvement in these wars was essentially defensive, the defence of her material bases of success at home and abroad and a defence of the traditional ideas of politics against the revolutionary fervour of France. The final defeat of Napoleon in 1814 and 1815 raised the question of Europe's future. The Vienna Settlement had as its primary aims the maintenance of peace and the self-interests of the individual states involved. There was some adjustment but not fundamental review of the territorial situation. Most importantly, it was essential that some balance of power be attained. The 'Congress-system' was the answer to these problems. It presupposed that confrontation between the major European powers should be replaced by co-operation.

Increasingly Britain found herself out of step with the reactionary interpretation of the Vienna Settlement which seemingly justified intervention in the affairs of states, generally the smaller and weaker ones, by the great powers to stifle liberalism and nationalism. This situation accounts for Castlereagh's State Paper of 1820. Yet Castlereagh was restating the long tradition of British foreign policy: that involvement and intervention in European affairs could have detrimental economic effects. British foreign policy reverted to the pragmatic and flexible approach which had characterised it in the eighteenth century. 'Nothing was immutable' in foreign policy, 'a settlement was only settled for as long as it was realistic' (P. Haynes, *The Nineteenth Century 1814–1880*). This view can be seen in all the documents. Palmerston and successive ministers may have used the language of moral imperatives but in practice their decisions were based not upon them but upon pragmatic analysis of advantage and disadvantage.

The expansion and consolidation of international trade for the benefit of Britain proved to be a more realistic and ultimately more important aim of foreign policy. Granville's statement in 1852 makes this clear. The idea of 'economic imperialism' was a major force in foreign policy formulation. These attitudes coloured Britain's attitude to Europe. Britain could not isolate herself totally from European affairs because of her substantial economic interests there. Europe remained throughout the nineteenth century the most important market for British manufactured goods. The dominance of Europe by one great power was potentially fatal to Britain's economic, political and strategic considerations.

The documents printed below provide the 'official' view of foreign policy principles. It is up to the student to apply them to specific problems, like Belgium, Turkey or China. They emphasise the continuity of thought behind political action.

Further Reading

For the beginner studying foreign policy there are three useful, up-to-date works which complement each other, all with useful bibliographies:

K. Bourne, *The Foreign Policy of Victorian England 1830–1902*, Oxford, 1970, documents and commentary

P. Haynes, *The Nineteenth Century 1814–1880*, London, 1975, which deals with foreign policy in terms of principle and action

A. J. Marcham, *Examining the Evidence: Foreign Policy*, Methuen, 1973

An alternative approach to foreign policy is through biography. The following will be found most useful:

J. W. Derry, *Castlereagh*, Allen Lane, 1976, based on earlier works with little new to say, but a good student synthesis

P. Dixon, *Canning: Politician and Statesman*, Weidenfeld and Nicolson, 1976

W. Hinde, *George Canning*, Collins, 1973

L. Iremonger, *Aberdeen*, 1978, a good biography of a somewhat maligned Foreign Secretary and Prime Minister

J. Prest, *Lord John Russell*, Macmillan, 1972, a sympathetic biography which deals less fully with his final years when he was Foreign Secretary than with his role in the 1830s

J. Ridley, *Lord Palmerston*, Constable, 1970, a magisterial biography and also a good read; Ridley adopts a pragmatic view of Palmerston's policies and this should be compared with Southgate's ideological stance

D. Southgate, '*The Most English minister*' – *the policies and politics of Palmerston*, Macmillan, 1966

1 The Foundations laid down – Castlereagh's Position

. . . It remains to be considered what course can best be pursued by the Allies in the present critical state of Europe, in order to preserve in the utmost cordiality and vigor, the Bonds which at this day so happily unite the Great European Powers together, and draw from their Alliance,
5 should the moment of danger and contest arrive, the fullest extent of belief, of which it is in its nature susceptible.

In this Alliance as in all human Arrangements, nothing is more likely to impair or even destroy its real utility, than any attempt to push it's duties and its obligations beyond the sphere which its original Conception and
10 understood principles will warrant:– It was a Union for the Re-Conquest and liberation of a great proportion of the Continent of Europe from the Military Dominion of France. . . . It was never however intended as a Union for the Government of the World, or for the superintendence of the internal Affairs of other States:– It provided
15 specifically against an infraction on the part of France of the State of possession then created:– It provided against the return of the Usurper or any of his Family to the throne:– It further designated the Revolutionary power which had convulsed France, and desolated Europe, as the object of it's constant solicitude; but it was the Revolutionary Power more
20 particularly in its Military Character actual and existent within France against which it intended to take precautions, and not against the Democratick Principles then as now, but too generally spread throughout Europe.

In thus attempting to limit the objects of the Alliance within their
25 legitimate Boundary, it is not meant to discourage the utmost Frankness of Communication between the Allies Cabinets. . . . It is not meant that in particular and definite Cases, the Alliance may not (and especially when invited to do so by the Parties interested) advantageously interpose, with Caution, in matters lying beyond the Boundaries of their immediate
30 and particular Connections; but what is intended to be combated as forming any part of their duty as Allies is, the notion, but too perceptibly prevalent, that whenever any great Political Event shall occur, as in Spain, pregnant enough with future danger, it is to be regarded as a matter of course, that it belongs to the Allies to charge themselves collectively with

35   the responsibility of exercising some Jurisdiction concerning such
possible eventual danger.

    One objection to this view of our duties, if there is no other, is that
unless we are prepared to support our interference with force our
judgement or advice is likely to be rarely listened to and would soon by
40   frequent repetition fall into complete contempt:— . . . The grounds of
the intervention thus become unpopular, the intention of the Parties is
misunderstood, the public Mind is agitated and perverted, and the
general Political situation of the Government is thereby essentially
embarrassed:—

45   This Statement is only meant to prove, that we ought to see somewhat
clearly to what purpose of real utility, our efforts tend, before we embark
on proceedings which can never be indifferent in their bearings upon the
Governments taking part in them — In this Country at all times, but
especially at the present Conjunction, when the whole energy of the State
50   is required to unite reasonable men in defence of our existing Institutions,
and put down the Spirit of Treason and disaffection which in certain of
the Manufacturing Districts in particular, pervades the Lower Orders, it
is of the greatest moment, that the Public Sentiment should not be
distracted or divided, by the unnecessary interference of the Government
55   in the events passing abroad, over which they can have none, or at best
imperfect, means of Controul:— Nothing could be more injurious to the
Continental Powers than to have their affairs made the matter of daily
discussion in our Parliament . . . .

    These considerations will suggest a doubt whether that extreme degree
60   of unanimity and supposed concurrence upon all political subjects, would
be either a practicable or a desirable Principle of action, among the Allied
States, upon matters not essentially connected with the main purposes of
the Alliance. . . . The Principle of one State interfering by force in the
internal affairs of another, in order to enforce obedience to the governing
65   authority is always a question of the greatest moral as well as political
delicacy. . . . It is only important on the present occasion to observe, that
to generalise such a Principle, and to think of reducing it to a system, or to
impose it as an obligation, is a scheme utterly impractical and
objectionable . . . .

          Castlereagh's State Paper of 5 May 1820, Public Record Office,
          F.O. 120/39/; printed in H.W.V. Temperley and L.M. Penson,
          Foundations of British Foreign Policy 1792—1902, London, 1966, pp
          48—63

Questions

a   (i) What was the 'present critical state of Europe' and what was the
    response of the allies to this (line 2)?
    (ii) What were 'original Conception and understood principles' (lines
    9—10) of the alliance?
    (iii) In lines 14—23, what does Castlereagh identify as the *raison d'etre*

for the alliance and what does he not see as its function? Why do you think he made this statement?

(iv) Explain the reference to Spain in line 32. In what ways was Castlereagh involved in this question?

(v) Explain Castlereagh's position on interference, expressed in lines 63–6.

b What were the new principles to which Castlereagh objected so much and why?

c Why did Castlereagh place great emphasis on the state of Britain in 1820 (lines 48–58) in his critique of the new principles of the alliance?

d What did Castlereagh mean by 'non-intervention'?

* e Given this statement of foreign policy is it still justifiable to see Castlereagh as the most 'European' of British statesmen?

* f Canning maintained that he adhered to the State Paper of 1820, at least in theory. How far did he differ from it in practice?

2 Palmerston's Viewpoint in the 1830s

. . . My . . . opinion has certainly not been shaken by the progress of events. Every day brings fresh proof of the complete union of the three powers on every question on European policy, and affords additional evidence that they are for the present what they told us three years ago
5 they must be considered – namely, a unity. Here is Austria setting at defiance the keen sympathy her Galician, Hungarian and Transylvanian subjects have openly manifested for the Poles, and making herself the tool to execute a measure of Russian vengeance, in which she herself has no interest whatever, or, rather, with respect to which her interests are
10 directly at variance with Russia. Her motive is obvious. She found Russia determined to execute the measure: she knew the consequences of a Russian occupation, and to avert that evil she chose rather to encounter the unpopularity of the act, and to perform it herself. But this is a fresh proof that in the present state of things we must not look to Metternich
15 for any co-operation in measures destined to hold Russia in check. He will edge away to us and France, if we and France boldly take up our own ground; but he will not, and cannot join us in the first instance.

The answer then which Austria will infallibly make you will be, that we all wish the same thing, and that therefore we ought to concert as to
20 the best means of obtaining our common object. That for this purpose we must establish a conference at some central place, and Vienna will be proposed as best suited for speedy communication with Petersburg, Constantinople, Berlin, Paris and London. Are we to accept such an offer or decline it? If we accept it we enter into a labyrinth of negotiation out of
25 which I see no clue. England and France will be in a minority. We were so about Belgium; but in that case the negotiations were in London, and the weight of a government on the spot speaking through its plenipotentiary gave that plenipotentiary double authority; while also England and

France being the two powers closest to Belgium, had on that account the greatest means of action in the country which was the subject of negotiation. The reverse of all this would happen with respect to the Vienna conference, and we should be dragged along with the other three against our opinions or else compelled to withdraw. But a conference broken up by disagreement does not leave the parties upon the same terms on which it found them at its commencement, and Europe would in such a case be still more divided into two camps than it is now. . . . The division of Europe into two camps, as Ancillon calls it, to which you so much object, is the result of events beyond our control, and is the consequence of the French Revolution of July. The three powers fancy their interest lies in the direction opposite to that in which we and France conceive ours to be placed. The separation is not one of words but of things; not the effect of caprice or of will, but produced by the force of occurrences. The three and two think differently, and therefore they act differently. . . . This separation cannot really cease to exist till all the questions to which it applies are decided — just as it is impossible to make a coalition ministry while there are questions pending on which public men disagree. But when Ancillon and Metternich complain of this division of Europe into two camps, that which they really complain of is, not the existence of two camps, but of the equality of the two camps. The plain English of it all is, that they want to have England on their side against France, that they may dictate terms to France as they did in 1814 and 1815; and they are provoked beyond measure at the steady protection which France has derived from us. But it is that protection which has preserved the peace of Europe. Without it there would long ago have been a general war.

> Private letter from Lord Palmerston to Lord Melbourne, 1 March 1836, in L. C. Sanders (ed.), *Lord Melbourne's Letters*, London, 1890, pp 337–40

Questions

a　(i) What were the 'three powers' to which Palmerston refers (lines 2– 3)? How accurate was his assessment of European Policy at this time?

(ii) Who was Metternich and why did Palmerston place little store by his attitude over Russian aggression (lines 14– 15)?

(iii) Explain the reference to Belgium (line 25). In what ways did this confirm Palmerston's attitude towards the European powers?

(iv) How does Palmerston explain the 'division of Europe into two camps' in lines 37– 44?

(v) In what ways does Palmerston see 'the steady protection which France has derived from us' (lines 52– 3) as the cause of this division? What other results does he see as deriving from that protection? Is his assessment valid?

b　What justification was there in the early 1830s for Palmerston to

argue that 'Every day brings fresh proof of the complete union of the
three powers on every question of European policy' (lines 2–3)?

c   How did Palmerston feel that the problems of Europe could be aired?
But what did he think the outcome would be and why?

d   Does Palmerston regard the division of Europe into two camps as
advantageous to Britain or not?

*   e   Palmerston argues that the division of Europe was 'the result of events
beyond our control, and is the consequence of the French Revolution
of July' (lines 38–9). What justifications are there for this statement?

*   f   How does this document help you to explain Palmerston's attitude to
Europe in the 1830s?

3   Palmerston as Successor to Castlereagh

(a) One of the general principles which Her Majesty's Government wish
to observe as a guide to their conduct in dealing with the relations
between England and other States, is, that changes which foreign Nations
may chuse to make in their internal Constitutions and form of
5   Government, are to be looked upon as matters with which England has
no business to interfere by force of arms, for the purpose of imposing
upon such Nations a Form of Government which they do not wish to
have, or for the purpose of preventing such Nations having Institutions
which they desire. These things are considered in England to be matters of
10   domestic concern, which every Nation ought to be allowed to settle as it
likes.

But an attempt of one Nation to seize and to appropriate to itself
territory which belongs to another Nation, is a different matter; because
such an attempt leads to a derangement of the existing Balance of Power,
15   and by altering the relative strength of States may tend to create danger to
other Powers; and such attempts therefore, the British Government holds
itself at full liberty to resist, upon the universally acknowledged principle
of self-defence.

Palmerston's dispatch no. 6 to the Marquess of Clanricarde,
20   ambassador in St Petersburg, 11 January 1841

(b) The principle on which I have thought the foreign policy of this
country ought to be conducted is the principle of maintaining peace and
friendly understandings with all nations, as long as it was possible to do so
consistently with a due regard to the interests, the honour, and the dignity
25   of this country. My endeavours have been to preserve peace. All the
Governments of which I have had the honour to be a Member have
succeeded in accomplishing that object. The main charges brought
against me are that I did not involve this country in perpetual quarrels
from one end of the globe to the other. . . . We have endeavoured to
30   extend the commercial relations of the country, or to place them where
extension was not required, on a firmer basis, and upon a footing of
greater security. . . . I hold with respect to alliances, that England is a

Power sufficiently strong, sufficiently powerful, to steer her own course, and not to tie herself as an unnecessary appendage to the policy of any other Government. I hold that the real policy of England . . . is to be the champion of justice and right; pursuing the course with prudence and moderation, not becoming the Quixote of the world, but giving the weight of her moral sanction and support wherever she thinks that justice is, and wherever she thinks that wrong has been done. . . . I would adopt the expression of Canning, and say that with every British Minister the interests of England ought to be the shibboleth of his policy.

Speech by Palmerston in the House of Commons, 1 March 1848

(c) We have shown that liberty is compatible with order; that individual freedom is reconcilable with obedience to the law. We have shown the example of a nation, in which every class of society accepts with cheerfulness the lot which Providence has assigned to it; while at the same time every individual of each class is constantly striving to raise himself in the social scale — not by injustice and wrong, not by violence and illegality — but by persevering good conduct, and by the steady and energetic exertion of the moral and intellectual faculties which his Creator has endowed him. . . . I therefore fearlessly challenge the verdict which this House, as representing a political, a commercial, a constitutional country, is to give on the question now brought before it; whether the principles on which the foreign policy of Her Majesty's Government has been conducted, and the sense of duty which has led us to think ourselves bound to afford protection to our fellow subjects abroad, are proper and fitting guides for those who are charged with the Government of England; and whether, as the Roman, in days of old, held himself free from indignity, when he could say *Civis Romanus sum*; so also a British subject, in whatever land he may be, shall feel confident that the watchful eye and the strong arm of England will protect him against injustice and wrong.

Palmerston's '*Civis Romanus sum*' speech, June 1850; fuller versions of these extracts are printed in K. Bourne, *The Foreign Policy of Victorian England 1830–1902*, Oxford, 1970, pp 252–4, 291–3, 301–2

Questions

a (i) In what circumstances would Palmerston countenance intervention and in what circumstances would he not (document 3(a))?
(ii) What does Palmerston see as the basis of England's policy abroad (document 3(b))? How does he feel that this policy should be implemented?
(iii) How far did Palmerston believe that a Briton could echo the Roman belief '*Civis Romanus sum*' (document 3(c), line 60)? In what ways did he show this in his policies in the 1850s?

b What does Palmerston see as the basic principles behind British foreign policy?

c In what circumstances did Palmerston see intervention as justifiable and why?

d In what ways are there basic inconsistencies in Palmerston's arguments over foreign policy in these three documents?

* *e* How far can Palmerston be said to be continuing the traditions of British foreign policy established by Castlereagh and Canning?

* *f* Palmerston viewed foreign policy in terms of moral absolutes and pragmatic principles. Discuss.

4 Policy re-iterated

. . . In the opinion of the Present Cabinet, it is the duty and the interest of this country, having possessions scattered over the whole globe, and priding itself on its advanced state of civilization, to encourage moral, intellectual and physical progress among all other nations.

5 For this purpose the Foreign Policy of Great Britain should be marked by justice, moderation, and self respect, and this country should in her relations with other States do by others as it would be done by. While the Cabinet do not believe that all considerations of a higher character are to be sacrificed to the pushing our manufactures by any means into every

10 possible corner of the globe yet considering the great natural advantage of our Foreign Commerce, and the powerful means of civilization it affords, one of the first duties of the British Govt must always be to obtain for our Foreign Trade that security which is essential to its success.

British subjects of all classes, engaged in innocent pursuits, are entitled

15 abroad as well as at home to the protection of their Govt. Where they have been treated with injustice, they have the right to expect that redress should be demanded ·in strong but dignified language, followed if necessary by corresponding measures; where they may, by their own wanton folly or misconduct, have got into difficulties in a Foreign land,

20 they have no right to expect assistance, and even where they unwittingly but imprudently subject themselves to the penal laws of the country in which they find themselves they can only claim those good offices, the efficacy of which must depend upon the friendliness of our relations with the country in which the difficulty has arisen.

25 The Cabinet adhere to the principle of non-intervention in the internal affairs of other countries. . . . They do not attach to the word 'non-intervention' the meaning implied by some who use it, viz. that Diplomacy is obsolete, and that it is unnecessary for this country to know, or take part in what passes in other countries. H.M.'s Govt ought to be

30 informed accurately and immediately, by their Agents, of every important event which may arise.

With regard to occurrences likely to have international consequences no general rule can uniformly be applied. In each case, the Govt must

exercise its own discretion, whether it shall interfere at once, or remain
35 aloof till its arbitration or good offices be required. The latter course may
often be advisable when, as at present, opinion abroad is in extremes, and
the Foreign Policy of England has obtained, whether justly or unjustly,
the reputation of interfering too much. It will also often be found
advisable to combine with other great powers, when no sacrifice of
40 principle is required, to settle the disputes which may arise between other
nations.

With respect to those internal arrangements of other countries, such as
the establishment of Liberal Institutions and the reduction of Tariffs, in
which this country has an indirect interest, H.M.'s Representatives ought
45 to be furnished with the views of H.M.'s Govt on each subject, and the
arguments best adapted to support those views, but they should at the
same time be instructed to press these views only when fitting
opportunities arise, and when their advice and assistance are
required. . . . H.M.'s Cabinet believe that every assistance, within the
50 one competency of Govt should be given to all those undertakings which
tend to promote a more rapid interchange of knowledge and opinions
among various countries; they believe that such increased intercourse will
tend more than anything else to promote the Peace of the World . . . .

Lord Granville's 'General Statement of Foreign Policy', 12
January 1852, Public Record Office 30/29/18 part I

Questions

a (i) What is the 'Present Cabinet' to which Granville refers (line 1)?
What does he see as the guiding force behind foreign policy (lines 1–
4, 12–15)?
(ii) What does Granville understand by 'non-intervention' (line 25)?
(iii) Explain Granville's assertion that 'the Foreign Policy of England
has . . . the reputation of interfering too much' (lines 37–38).

b What ideal aims does Granville see for foreign policy and what more
practical aspects does he identify? Which do you think was considered
more important by contemporaries and why?

c How does Granville's interpretation of the right of foreign nationals
differ from Palmerston's?

d Does Granville's view of 'non-intervention' follow the already
established traditions of foreign policy?

* e How far can Granville's view of foreign policy be said to be
Palmerstonian but without the 'gunboats'?

* f By 1850 economic considerations were the dominant element in
British foreign policy. Discuss.

Further Work

a 'British Foreign Ministers have been guided by what seemed to them
to be the immediate interest of this Country without making
elaborate calculations for the future.' (Viscount Grey of Fallodon,

Twenty-Five Years, London, 1925, i, p 6). How far does analysis of foreign policy between 1812 and 1865 substantiate this statement?

b   How far are the personalities involved in foreign policy of importance in understanding developments in the 1820–65 period?

c   Economic expansion was a far more important objective of British foreign policy than any other objective. How far is this statement justifiable?

d   What problems of historical method does the historian have to face in analysing foreign policy in this period?

VIII   Egypt and the 'Scramble for Africa'

Introduction

The 'Scramble for Africa' of the late nineteenth century took place when British pre-eminence in the world was ebbing; admittedly the greatest extent of British domination lay in the future, and true imperialism was more a feature of the early twentieth century. It was in 1907 that Lord Curzon said, 'Imperialism is . . . animated by the supreme idea. . . . To the people of the mother state it must be a discipline, an inspiration and a faith. . . . To the people of the circumference . . . it must give them . . . the sense of partnership in a great idea, the consecrating influence of a lofty purpose.' But Britain's mid-Victorian 'informal Empire' based on free trade was giving way in the 1870s and 1880s to partition and annexation. Motives for this are, apparently, endless, but several historians emphasise the role of the British occupation of Egypt in 1882 in stimulating colonial activity elsewhere in Africa. Robinson and Gallagher's thesis is here represented by their most recent contribution, while suggestions against its validity are offered by Sanderson. Traditional historiography stresses the importance of European dip-lomacy and economics (e.g. in Disraeli's acquisition of the Khedive's mortgaged Canal shares in 1875), and the importance of Bismarck to the Egyptian crisis is shown here.

However, the rise of the 'Third World' in the mid-twentieth century has meant increasing demands to view the Scramble from the African point of view. As one reviewer regretfully wrote in 1975, 'Europeans are . . . always the agents of rationality and modernization, while Africans and Asians represent conservative "pre-capitalist" modes of behaviour.' Robinson's 'excentric' (the title is his) theory is one step towards indicating the role of the indigenous population in the Scramble.

No attempt is made here to examine the theoretical nature of 'capitalist imperialism', nor to survey the vast range of activities in Africa and Europe which inspired or induced the partition. Rather, the documents indicate the way in which one event — the British occupation of Egypt — has been held to have begun the partition, and how historians' views can change; Robinson is more reticent (in his recent work) on the effect of Egypt on the Scramble. It is essential for students to have read thoroughly about the events of the Egyptian problem. before tackling these documents, and to think widely about the effects of the 1882 crisis. What were the effects, if any, in East and South Africa? What were British fears about Egypt, and were they well-founded? Was Egypt *sui generis*, not classifiable with other parts of Africa, even in the North? The debate continues.

Further Reading

M. E. Chamberlain, *The New Imperialism*, Historical Association pamphlet, 1970, a brief description of the events and historiography of the 'Scramble' in Africa and China

M. E. Chamberlain, *The Scramble for Africa*, Longman, 1974, a documentary collection with introductory chapters, on the lines of her earlier pamphlet

D. K. Fieldhouse, *Economics and Empire 1830–1914*, Weidenfeld and Nicolson, 1973, a very readable guide to economic imperialism, with case-studies from Africa and the Far East

H. Gollwitzer, *Europe in the Age of Imperialism 1880–1914*, Thames and Hudson, 1969, useful on the European context of imperialism, with many illustrations

R. Oliver and A. Atmore, *Africa since 1800*, Cambridge University Press, 1972, the best concise, factual account of events

R. Robinson and J. Gallagher, *Africa and the Victorians*, Macmillan, 1961, the 'Egyptocentric' argument in its purest form: controversial and stimulating

1 The Suez Canal

The Suez Canal, which had been opened in 1869, cut the distance from Britain to India by several weeks and some thousands of miles. In 1875 four-fifths of its traffic was British. . . . Moreover, its strategic importance was even greater than its commercial. In the event of another Indian
5 Mutiny, or an invasion by Russia, the Suez Canal could carry reinforcements far more quickly than the old Cape route. . . . 'It is now [as Cairns wrote to Disraeli in January 1876] the *Canal and India*; there is no such thing now to us as India alone . . . .'

Most of the Egyptian lands were in French hands. So were all the
10 founders' shares and 56 per cent of the ordinary shares of the Suez Canal Company. The remainder of the ordinary shares belonged to the Khedive, who had, however, mortgaged them until 1895. It seemed all too likely that if the Khedive, whose financial profligacy was only surpassed by that of his nominal suzerain, the Sultan, finally went
15 bankrupt, the French Government would seize the chance of intervening, and would be in a position to threaten a vital British interest . . . .

On November 14th [1875, Disraeli] wrote in triumph to Queen Victoria:

. . . It is just settled; you have it, Madam. The French Government has been
20 out-generalled. They tried too much, offering loans at an usurious rate, and
with conditions which would have virtually given them the government of
Egypt.
     The Khedive, in despair and disgust offered your Majesty's Government to
purchase his shares outright . . . .

25 Disraeli's coup was widely heralded as a new departure in foreign
policy. Particularly in Liberal circles it was expected to foreshadow a
British occupation of Egypt; Cairo would replace Constantinople as the
key to India, and the odious task of bolstering up Turkey would be
abandoned. Right-wing Liberals, like Hartington and Goschen wel-
30 comed what they believed to be imminent, while Tory diehards uttered
warnings against abandoning the old Crimean policy. Britain did in the
end occupy Egypt and give up the effort to defend Turkey, but no such
intention existed in Disraeli's mind at the time. Historians who have seen
in his action a deeply matured plan which came to fruition later are in
35 error. Although there would have been much to be said for such a change
of policy, all the evidence points to Disraeli's determination to adhere to
the traditional course. It wás months after the Suez purchase that he
disclaimed . . . any intention to substitute the annexation of Egypt for
the integrity of Turkey, and throughout his period in office he
40 consistently refused to be drawn by Bismarck into the Egyptian
imbroglio.
     His objective was rather to forestall France and prevent a French
occupation than to take any step towards seizing Egypt for Britain. No
doubt with his capacity to dramatize events he wished it to be believed,
45 even believed himself, that he had done much more and that somehow
the Canal had actually fallen into British hands. The facts cannot sustain
this fantasy. Derby stated them more correctly in a speech at Edinburgh,
to the annoyance of the Queen, who considered that he had 'tried to pour
as much cold water as he could on the great success'. We were acting, he
50 said, simply to prevent a great highway filled with our shipping coming
under the exclusive control 'of the foreign shareholders of a foreign
company'. But it was Disraeli's more colourful version that got the ear of
Europe and of posterity. And so a new historical myth came into being
half consciously fabricated by the most potent myth-maker in British
55 history.
          R. Blake, *Disraeli*, 1966, pp 581—2, 584, 586—7

Questions

a Why was the Canal important to Britain?
b Who was the 'Khedive' (line 12)?
c Who was Britain's main rival in Egypt?
d What does Disraeli's letter suggest about his relationship with Queen
   Victoria?

    e   What was 'the old Crimean policy' (line 31)? Was Disraeli still maintaining it?

*   *f*   Did the events of 1875 lead inevitably to those of 1882?

2   Bismarck and the Eastern Question

The Eastern policy of England he [Bismarck] believed to be based on the absolute necessity to keep the road to India free, the earnest desire to maintain the political *status quo* in Turkey, in Asia, and in Egypt, and the philanthropic wish to improve the material condition of the Sultan's
5 subjects. His Majesty had, therefore, every reason to confide and rely in the policy of England, whilst Germany had every reason to support that policy, because it was conducive to the maintenance of peace and order in Europe.

    He looked upon the breaking up of the Turkish Empire as so great a
10 danger to Europe, that he was prepared to go great lengths to keep it together, at least as long as he lived himself, for what happened after his death he had no means of controlling, and as the Turks, as a military nation, had proved themselves to be the race best able to keep order among the various nationalities composing the Empire, he would support
15 the Turkish Government for the sake of keeping the Empire together.

    In regard to Egypt, he also agreed with England, that the *status quo* should be maintained, and he thought England right to resist the interference of any other Power in Egypt, and he held that England would be justified in going to war to resist any foreign interference with
20 Egypt, and if ever he should be consulted about a foreign occupation of Egypt, he would give his opinion in favour of a Turkish occupation, and would object to any other but a Turkish garrison for Egypt.

    He agreed in all points with the policy of England, except in one, and that was, the philanthropic side of her policy. He believed that pressure
25 for reforms could be overdone, and actually did more harm than good, because the irritation produced on the Turkish mind by high foreign pressure manifested itself by increased procrastination, and led to the very result it was so desirable to obviate.

    He could, therefore, not give his support to a policy of pressure for
30 reforms, and believed that better results could be obtained by leaving the Sultan alone, and giving the Pashas time to reflect on the advice already tendered by the Powers since the Congress of Berlin which, he flattered himself, had really laid the foundation of lasting peace in Turkey.

    I thanked Prince Bismarck for his friendly communication, and said
35 that he had rightly interpreted our policy in regard to the road to India, and the maintenance of the political *status quo* in Turkey, Asia, and Egypt; but that we could never cease to press for reforms in Turkey, and for the improvement of the condition of the Sultan's subjects, because we knew from experience that if we ever relaxed our efforts, the Ottoman
40 Administration would become more corrupt, and the condition of the

people more abject and hopeless than it was even now . . . .

> Lord Ampthill to Earl Granville, 20 December 1881, Cabinet
> Memoranda 37/6/36, quoted in C. J. Lowe, *The Reluctant
> Imperialists*, Vol II, 1967, pp 9 – 11

Questions

a   Explain 'philanthropic' (line 4), 'Pashas' (line 31), '*status quo*' (line 3).
b   What did Bismarck see as Britain's Eastern policy?
c   Why does Bismarck disagree with Britain's philanthropy? How does
      Ampthill reply?
*   *d*   How did the Congress of Berlin (1878) affect the situation in the
      Eastern Mediterranean?
*   *e*   What foreign power had interests in Egypt, other than Britain? What
      were those interests?
*   *f*   What action did Bismarck take when the British occupied Egypt in
      1882? What was the '*bâton égyptien*'?

3   Egypt and the 'Scramble'

The partition of the African tropics which began [in 1883] . . . was not
the result of the Tunisian mishap, or of Leopold's schemes and Bismarck's
wiles, or of the squabbles of white merchants and explorers on the spot.
What drove it on was the Suez crisis and the repercussions of that
5   crisis . . . .
     The shots of Seymour at Alexandria and Wolseley at Tel el Kebir were
to echo round the world. It transpired in the end that their *ricochets* had
blown Africa into the modern age. The onslaught on Arabia opened the
long Anglo–French conflict over Egypt which more than anything
10   brought on the division of East and West Africa. . . . To the French, the
veiled protectorate was the worst humiliation since Sedan. Their canal
and the country which they had nursed since Napoleon's landing had
been snatched away under their very noses. This broke the Liberal *entente*
and kept Britain and France at odds for twenty years. Once in Egypt,
15   moreover, Britain became highly vulnerable to continental diplomacy.
To set Egyptian finances in order, she needed German support against
French vetoes in the Debt Commission. . . . By altering European
alignments thus, the Egyptian occupation for the rest of the century gave
the powers both incentive and opportunity to break the traditional
20   understandings about tropical Africa.

> R. E. Robinson and J. Gallagher, 'The Partition of Africa', in
> F. H. Hinsley (ed.), *The New Cambridge Modern History, Volume
> XI, Material Progress and World-Wide Problems, 1870–98*, 1962,
> pp 597, 601 – 2

Questions

a   What were the 'Tunisian mishap' and 'Leopold's schemes' (line 2)?
b   The authors emphasise the importance of the Suez crisis. What arguments do they use to support this?
*   c   How is this extract related to Ampthill's conversation with Bismarck? (See document 2.)
d   'Liberal *entente*' (line 13), 'traditional understandings' (lines 19—20). What do these suggest about mid-Victorian imperialism?
e   What evidence is there in the extract that French imperialism was largely a question of prestige?
*   f   Trace the connection between the various parts of Africa in the early 1880s mentioned in the extract.

4   A Critique of the Strategic Theory

[According to Robinson and Gallagher] the process of partition begins when a European Power (Britain) reluctantly saddles itself with new territorial responsibilities in Africa in order to defend the strategic security of older imperial possessions. But this move injures the interests
5   of another Power (France) which retorts by counter-annexations, some of them merely as 'compensation', but others intended also as a strategic threat to Britain's new African acquisitions. Britain then seeks security for these new acquisitions by yet further strategic annexations. Meanwhile, other Powers exploit the rivalry of France and Britain to make
10   annexations of their own, some of which are also strategically dangerous to Britain.

   This model seems at first sight to work admirably in the Nile Valley, where in 1882 the British occupied Egypt primarily to safeguard the Suez route to India, thereby provoking (but surely rather belatedly?) a French
15   strategic challenge to the security of the waters of the Upper Nile and so to the security of Egypt itself. To this challenge, in both its potential and its actual phases, the British responded by a variety of diplomatic and military expedients designed to halt the French at Egypt's 'new frontiers of insecurity' in the remote fastnesses of East and Central Africa.
20   Meanwhile, in the early stages of the Anglo-French dispute, Leopold II and Bismarck had seized the opportunity to stake their claims . . . .

   The strategic theory . . . encounters difficulties in the overwhelming importance which it attributes to the Egyptian situation both as initiator of the partition and as the main drive behind its explosive extension.
25   'When the British entered Egypt on their own, the scramble began.' [Robinson and Gallagher] But did it? Whenever the partition of tropical Africa began, it was not in 1882 or 1883. By 1882—3 it was already well under way, with the French conquest of the Senegal hinterland already fully launched, the British and French actively competing for territory on
30   the West Coast, and the French confronting King Leopold on the Congo.

Moreover, in West Africa proper, the crucial French decisions to go forward had been taken as early as 1879–80 . . . .

'From start to finish the partition of tropical Africa was driven by the persistent crisis in Egypt.' [Robinson and Gallagher] But was it? The
35 Egyptian crisis did not initiate the partition; nor, down to mid-1884, did it have much discernible effect in driving on a partition that had already begun. French expansion in West Africa, in particular, had a dynamic that was quite independent of the Egyptian situation. From 1879 to about the end of 1883, when there was no Anglo-French quarrel in Egypt, or
40 none that the Quai d'Orsay would recognise, it had gone ahead very rapidly. In 1884–5, just when the Egyptian quarrel became open and embittered, it slowed down almost to a standstill. Enormous expenditure, and military setbacks both in the Niger Sudan and elsewhere, created a mood of disillusionment with overseas expansion; the 'official mind' even
45 began to wonder whether some of the recent acquisitions were really worth the expense of obtaining them.

> G. N. Sanderson, 'The European Partition of Africa: Coincidence or Conjuncture?', in *Journal of Imperial and Commonwealth History*, III (1974), pp 4–7

Questions

* *a* Has Sanderson in his first paragraph fairly summarised the views of Robinson and Gallagher (see document 3)?
* *b* What claims had Leopold II and Bismark staked?
  c Why does Sanderson not accept the 'strategic theory' (line 22)?
* *d* What was the 'official mind' of imperialism (line 44)?
* *e* French forward movement in Senegal was certainly in evidence before 1882, but does its existence disprove the 'strategic theory'?
* *f* What was the French 'strategic challenge to the security of the waters of the Upper Nile' (line 15)?

5 The Local Crisis

Imperialism in the industrial era is a process whereby agents of an expanding society gain inordinate influence or control over the vitals of weaker societies by 'dollar' and 'gun-boat' diplomacy, ideological suasion, conquest and rule, or by planting colonies of its own people
5 abroad. The object is to shape or reshape them in its own interest and more or less its own image. It implies the exertion of power and the transfer of economic resources; but no society, however dominant, can man-handle arcane, densely-populated civilisations or white colonies in other continents simply by projecting its own main force upon
10 them. . . . From beginning to end imperialism was a product of interaction between European and extra-European politics. European economic and strategic expansion took imperial form when these two

components operated at cross-purposes with the third and non-European component – that of indigenous collaboration and resistance. . . .
15 Without the voluntary or enforced co-operation of their governing élites, economic resources could not be transferred, strategic interests protected or xenophobic reaction and traditional resistance to change contained. Nor without indigenous collaboration, when the time came for it, could Europeans have conquered and ruled their non-European
20 empires . . . .

Sooner or later collaborating Oriental regimes fell into the international bankruptcy court as did the Ottoman Sultan and Egyptian Khedive in 1876. . . . One by one they became bones of contention between European powers, subjected to increasing foreign interference to
25 reform the management of their internal financial and political affairs. At this point Europe had forced its internal collaborators to play for high stakes with too few cards. Its demands were cutting off their regimes from the loyalty of the traditional élites which formerly upheld them . . . until eventually popular xenophobic, neotraditional uprisings
30 confronted their impotence. . . . More often than not it was this non-European component of European expansion that necessitated the extension of colonial empires in the last two decades of the nineteenth century and the first decade of the twentieth . . . .

Certainly a breakdown of this kind was the imperative behind the
35 British occupation of Egypt in 1882 and therefore incidentally for much of the subsequent rivalry impelling the partition of Africa . . . .

It was the crisis in Egyptian government provoked by heavier collaborative demands, rather than rivalry in Europe, which first set Britain and France competing for the advantage under the new
40 arrangements; and the lack of reliable Egyptian collaborators, rather than the fear of France or any increased interest in Egypt, which brought the redcoats onto the Suez Canal in 1882 and kept them there until 1956.

R. Robinson, 'Non-European foundations of European imperialism: sketch for a theory of collaboration', in R. Owen and B. Sutcliffe (eds), *Studies in the theory of imperialism*, 1972, pp 118–20, 130–1

Questions

a Explain ' "gun-boat" diplomacy' (line 3), 'ideological suasion' (lines 3–4), 'xenophobic reaction' (line 17).
b What point is Robinson making in his definition of imperialism?
c Who were the collaborators? Why, like the Khedive in 1876, did they lose their value?
* d Comparing this extract with p. 85 does it seem that Robinson has modified his earlier views on the effect of the Egyptian crisis?
* e Does the excentric theory explain how or why countries were interested in expansion, or what control was wanted for?

IX Victorian Trilogy

Introduction

Disraeli's scepticism, his biographer Robert Blake tells us, makes him 'a less "dated" figure than almost any contemporary politician. Morally and intellectually Gladstone was his superior. In courage, great though Disraeli's was, Gladstone was certainly not his inferior. But he was, far more than Disraeli, a man of his times. It is hard to imagine him living in any other period, whereas it is quite easy to envisage Disraeli living either today or in the era of Lord North.' These two great political figures, and the queen they served, dominate English history in the second half of the nineteenth century and remind us of the necessity in history to study personalities. The historical biography is a valued secondary source and, like all primary and secondary sources, requires to be asked questions and assessed. This section, unlike the other nine, is therefore based wholly on secondary sources.

The different personalities and political viewpoints of Gladstone and Disraeli — 'the Professor' and 'the old Jew' as Bismarck referred to them — are illustrated by the agitation over massacres in the Turkish empire in 1876 and by general comments on their foreign policies. Similar comparisons could be made by investigating how they tackled domestic problems — political and social — and imperial affairs. The fascinating role of the monarch — a shadow of the institution it had once been but a very substantial shadow in the person of Queen Victoria — in this 'classic age' of party strife before universal adult suffrage also adds to the period's interest. It may be asked what has caused the changes in politics over the last hundred years: there was no lack of enthusiasm in the combat of these two political giants in parliament or in the country, as Gladstone's 1879 Midlothian campaign demonstrated.

The personality contrast between these two can be succinctly put in their response to being offered the post of Prime Minister in 1868. Disraeli said, 'Yes! I have climbed to the top of the greasy pole.' Gladstone wrote in his diary, 'I ascend a steepening path with a burden ever gathering weight. The Almighty seems to sustain and spare me for some purpose of His own, deeply unworthy as I know myself to be. Glory be to His name!'

Further Reading

P. Adelman, *Gladstone, Disraeli and Later Victorian Politics*, Longman,

1970, a documentary collection on the issues involving the two rivals, with a good section on the parties

B. Disraeli, *Coningsby* (1844); *Sybil* (1845); *Lothair* (1870); readable as novels, as well as for insights into the period and the author

W. E. Gladstone, *Midlothian Speeches 1879*, (ed.) M.R.D. Foot, Leicester University Press, 1971, Gladstonian rhetoric at its apogee

E. Longford, *Victoria R. I.*, Weidenfeld and Nicolson, 1964

* R. T. Shannon, *Gladstone and the Bulgarian Agitation 1876*, Nelson, 1963, a good monograph

A. Trollope, *Phineas Finn* (1869); and his other political novels *Can you Forgive Her* (1864); *The Eustace Diamonds* (1873); *Phineas Redux* (1874); *The Prime Minister* (1876); *The Duke's Children* (1880).

One of the best documents on Disraeli is his former home, Hughenden Manor, Buckinghamshire, now owned by the National Trust.

1   The Queen and her Prime Ministers

. . . A new scene opened; and new protagonists – Mr Gladstone and Mr Disraeli – struggled together in the limelight. Victoria, from her post of vantage, watched these developments with that passionate and personal interest which she invariably imported into politics. Her prepossessions
5   were of an unexpected kind. Mr Gladstone had been the disciple of her revered Peel, and had won the approval of Albert; Mr Disraeli had hounded Sir Robert to his fall with hideous virulence, and the Prince had pronounced that he 'had not one single element of a gentleman in his composition'. Yet she regarded Mr Gladstone with a distrust and dislike
10   which steadily deepened, while upon his rival she lavished an abundance of confidence, esteem, and affection such as Lord Melbourne himself had hardly known.

Her attitude towards the Tory Minister had suddenly changed when she found that he alone among public men had divined her feelings at
15   Albert's death. Of the others she might have said 'they pity me and not my grief'; but Mr Disraeli had understood; and all his condolences had taken the form of reverential eulogies of the departed. The Queen declared that he was 'the only person who appreciated the Prince' . . . .

. . . Mr Gladstone, with his daemonic energy and his powerful
20   majority in the House of Commons, was irresistible; and for five years (1869–74) Victoria found herself condemned to live in an agitating atmosphere of interminable reform – reform in the Irish Church and the Irish land system, reform in education, reform in parliamentary elections, reform in the organization of the Army and the Navy, reform in the
25   administration of justice. She disapproved, she struggled, she grew very angry; she felt that if Albert had been living things would never have happened so; but her protests and her complaints were alike unavailing. The mere effort of grappling with the mass of documents which poured in upon her in an ever-growing flood was terribly exhausting. When the

30 draft of the lengthy and intricate Irish Church Bill came before her, accompanied by an explanatory letter from Mr Gladstone covering a dozen closely-written quarto pages, she almost despaired. She turned from the Bill to the explanation, and from the explanation back again to the Bill, and she could not decide which was the most confusing. . . .

35 　Unacceptable as Mr Gladstone's policy was, there was something else about him which was even more displeasing to Victoria. She disliked his personal demeanour towards herself. It was not that Mr Gladstone, in his intercourse with her, was in any degree lacking in courtesy or respect. On the contrary, an extraordinary reverence permeated his manner, both in

40 his conversation and his correspondence with the Sovereign. Indeed, with that deep and passionate conservatism which, to the very end of his incredible career, gave such an unexpected colouring to his inexplicable character, Mr Gladstone viewed Victoria through a haze of awe which was almost religious — as a sacrosanct embodiment of venerable

45 traditions — a vital element in the British Constitution — a Queen by Act of Parliament. But unfortunately the lady did not appreciate the compliment. The well-known complaint — 'He speaks to me as if I were a public meeting' — whether authentic or no — and the turn of the sentence is surely a little too epigrammatic to be genuinely Victorian —

50 undoubtedly expresses the essential element of her antipathy. She had no objection to being considered as an institution; she was one, and she knew it. But she was a woman too, and to be considered *only* as an institution — that was unbearable. And thus all Mr Gladstone's zeal and devotion, his ceremonious phrases, his low bows, his punctilious

55 correctitudes, were utterly wasted; and when, in the excess of his loyalty, he went further, and imputed to the object of his veneration, with obsequious blindness, the subtlety of intellect, the wide reading, the grave enthusiasm, which he himself possessed, the misunderstanding became complete. The discordance between the actual Victoria and this strange

60 Divinity made in Mr Gladstone's image produced disastrous results. Her discomfort and dislike turned at last into positive animosity, and, though her manners continued to be perfect, she never for a moment unbent; while he on his side was overcome with disappointment, perplexity, and mortification . . . .

65 　Then [from 1874] there followed six years of excitement, of enchantment, of felicity, of glory, of romance. The amazing being [Disraeli], who now at last, at the age of seventy, after a lifetime of extraordinary struggle, had turned into reality the absurdest of his boyhood's dreams, knew well enough to make his own, with absolute

70 completeness, the heart of the Sovereign Lady whose servant, and whose master, he had so miraculously become. In women's hearts he had always read as in an open book. . . . He surveyed what was before him with the eye of a past-master; and he was not for a moment at a loss. He realized everything — the interacting complexities of circumstances and charac-

75 ter, the pride of place mingled so inextricably with personal arrogance, the superabundant emotionalism, the ingenuousness of outlook, the solid,

the laborious respectability, shot through so incongruously by tempe-
ramental cravings for the coloured and the strange, the singular
intellectual limitations, and the mysteriously essential female element
impregnating every partiçle of the whole. A smile hovered over his
impassive features, and he dubbed Victoria 'the Faery'. The name
delighted him, for, with the epigrammatic ambiguity so dear to his heart,
it precisely expressed his vision of the Queen. The Spenserian allusion was
very pleasant – the elegant evocation of Gloriana; but there was more in
it than that: there was the suggestion of a diminutive creature, endowed
with magical – and mythical – properties, and a portentousness almost
ridiculously out of keeping with the rest of her make-up. The Faery, he
determined, should henceforward wave her wand for him alone. . . . He
was nothing if not personal; and he had perceived that personality was the
key that opened the Faery's heart. Accordingly, he never for a moment
allowed his intercourse with her to lose the personal tone; he invested all
the transactions of State with the charms of familiar conversation; she was
always the royal lady, the adored and revered mistress, he the devoted and
respectful friend. When once the personal relation was firmly established,
every difficulty disappeared. But to maintain that relation unin-
terruptedly in a smooth and even course a particular care was necessary:
the bearings had to be most assiduously oiled. Nor was Disraeli in any
doubt as to the nature of the lubricant. 'You have heard me called a
flatterer,' he said to Matthew Arnold, 'and it is true. Everyone likes
flattery; and when you come to royalty you should lay it on with a
trowel.' He practised what he preached. His adulation was incessant, and
he applied it in the very thickest slabs. 'There is no honour and no
reward,' he declared,

> that with him can ever equal the possession of your Majesty's kind thoughts.
> All his own thoughts and feelings and duties and affections are now
> concentrated in your Majesty, and he desires nothing more for his remaining
> years than to serve your Majesty, or, if that service ceases, to live on its memory
> as a period of his existence most interesting and fascinating . . . .

As for Victoria, she accepted everything – compliments, flatteries,
Elizabethan prerogatives – without a single qualm. After the long gloom
of her bereavement, after the chill of the Gladstonian discipline, she
expanded to the rays of Disraeli's devotion like a flower in the sun. The
change in her situation was indeed miraculous. No longer was she obliged
to puzzle for hours over the complicated details of business, for now she
had only to ask Mr Disraeli for an explanation, and he would give it her in
the most concise, in the most amusing, way. No longer was she worried
by alarming novelties; no longer was she put out at finding herself
treated, by a reverential gentleman in high collars, as if she were some
embodied precedent, with a recondite knowledge of Greek. And her de-
liverer was surely the most fascinating of men. The strain of charlatanism,
which had unconsciously captivated her in Napoleon III, exercised the
same enchanting effect in the case of Disraeli. Like a dram-drinker, whose

ordinary life is passed in dull sobriety, her unsophisticated intelligence
gulped down his rococo allurements with peculiar zest. She became
intoxicated, entranced. Believing all that he told her of herself, she
25 completely regained the self-confidence which had been slipping away
from her throughout the dark period that followed Albert's death. She
swelled with a new elation, while he, conjuring up before her wonderful
Oriental visions, dazzled her eyes with an imperial grandeur of which she
had only dimly dreamed....

30   ... her most valued gifts were the bunches of spring flowers which,
gathered by herself and her ladies in the woods at Osborne, marked in an
especial manner the warmth and tenderness of her sentiments. Among
these it was, he declared, the primroses that he loved the best. They were,
he said, 'the ambassadors of Spring', 'the gems and jewels of Nature'. He
35 liked them, he assured her, 'so much better for their being wild; they seem
an offering from the Fauns and Dryads of Osborne.' 'They show,' he told
her, 'that your Majesty's sceptre has touched the enchanted Isle.' He sat at
dinner with heaped-up bowls of them on every side. . . . She sent him
snowdrops, and his sentiment overflowed into poetry. 'Yesterday eve,' he
40 wrote,

there appeared, in Whitehall Gardens, a delicate-looking case, with a royal
superscription, which, when he opened, he thought, at first, that your Majesty
had graciously bestowed upon him the stars of your Majesty's principal orders.
And indeed, he was so impressed with this graceful illusion, that, having a
45 banquet, where there were many stars and ribbons, he could not resist the
temptation, by placing some snowdrops on his heart, of showing that he, too,
was decorated by a gracious Sovereign.
    Then, in the middle of the night, it occurred to him, that it might all be an
enchantment, and that, perhaps, it was a Faery gift and came from another
50 monarch: Queen Titania, gathering flowers, with her Court, in a soft and sea-
girt isle, and sending magic blossoms, which, they say, turn the heads of those
who receive them.
    Lytton Strachey, *Queen Victoria*, 1921, Penguin edn 1971, pp
    193, 195—8, 202—3, 205—8

Questions

a Identify 'her revered Peel (lines 5—6), Albert (line 6), Lord
    Melbourne (line 11), Napoleon III (line 121), Osborne (line 136).
b What transformed Victoria's attitude to Disraeli? How did he
    develop his relationship with the queen?
c Why did the queen dislike Gladstone?
* *d* What aspects of Victoria's life illustrate lines 74—80?
e What insight into Disraeli's personality do we obtain from these
    extracts?
f Do you think that the portrayal of the queen and these two Prime
    Ministers by Strachey is effective?

2   The Bulgarian Horrors

Gladstone wrote the pamphlet [*The Bulgarian Horrors and the Question of the East*] in three days while in bed with lumbago. The sensation was tremendous: 40,000 copies were sold in a week, 200,000 by the end of the month. His arguments have often been summarized and his famous peroration often quoted; though, in fact, by giving the impression that Gladstone wanted the whole Turkish population, not simply the apparatus of government, to be evicted from Europe his grand finale spoiled his own case.

> Let the Turks now carry away their abuses in the only possible way, namely by carrying off themselves. Their Zaptiehs and their Mudirs, their Bimbashis and their Yuzbachis, their Kaimakams and their Pashas, one and all, bag and baggage shall, I hope, clear out from the province they have desolated and profaned. . . . There is not a criminal in an Europe gaol, there is not a cannibal in the South Sea Islands whose indignation would not arise and overboil at the recital of that which has been done. . . . If it be allowable that the executive power of Turkey should renew at this great crisis, by permission or authority of Europe, the charter of its existence in Bulgaria, then there is not on record since the beginnings of political society a protest that man has lodged against intolerable misgovernment or a stroke that he has dealt at loathsome tyranny, that ought not henceforth to be branded as a crime.

Why did Gladstone intervene at this particular moment? The suggestion that he acted prematurely and should have awaited the appearance of Baring's full report has no justification. On August 29 the *Daily News* published a preliminary report by the American Consul General Schuyler, which, coming from a source of unimpeachable detachment, gave Gladstone ample evidence on which to base his pamphlet. Nor was it a case of political opportunism in any ordinary sense of the word. His action did, it is true, bring about by a series of almost inevitable steps his resumption in 1880 of the leadership of the Liberal party. Hartington's mistress, the German-born Duchess of Manchester, anxious for her lover's prospect of the Premiership, told Disraeli some weeks earlier at the end of the session: 'That gentleman is only waiting to come to the fore with all his hypocritical retirement.' And it is certainly true that for a man who had resigned as leader in 1875 because he 'deeply desired an interval between Parliament and the grave', Gladstone had been surprisingly active. But, although his latest move only confirmed the Duchess, along with most of the upper class, in their belief, Gladstone was not a hypocrite. He certainly had no intention of ousting Granville and Hartington, even if he was not very considerate in his treatment of them. Nor can the timing of his intervention be explained by the imminence of a by-election for the Buckinghamshire county seat made vacant by Disraeli's peerage. The home counties were the least 'atrocitarian' constituencies in the country, and the Rothschilds, hitherto pillars of Buckinghamshire Liberalism, seceded, approving, like most of English Jewry, of the Government's Turkish policy.

The truth is that Gladstone was swept into the main current belatedly, reluctantly and scarcely knowing where he was going. The idea that he had long been watching for the appropriate occasion and that his action was a superb example of 'right timing' has been effectively demolished; likewise Buckle's picture of him stalking Disraeli, like an 'old hunter, once more sniffing the scent' and seizing his opportunity. On the contrary Gladstone was slow to act, and his pamphlet came out long after the agitation had been gaining momentum. As the leading authority puts it, the episode was 'less a case of Gladstone exciting popular passion than of popular passion exciting Gladstone'. Gladstone had retired from the leadership of the Liberal party because the defeat of 1874 seemed to him a clear sign that he had lost that understanding with the virtuous masses, which since the 'sixties had been the inspiration of his political life. Suddenly, and surprisingly late in the day, he saw that the atrocity agitation might recover it for him. This was what he meant when he wrote that 'the game was afoot and the question still alive' or even more significantly on August 29 to Granville: 'Good ends can rarely be attained in politics without passion: and there is now, the first time for a good many years, a virtuous passion.' For Gladstone politics was a moral crusade based on the highest instincts of British democracy; or it was nothing. In the sense that he saw an opportunity of taking part in just such a moral crusade, he might be described as an opportunist, but not in any other sense.

Gladstone wholly lacked Disraeli's acute, though sporadic, comprehension of the material needs of the working class. Bread and butter politics were of no interest to him, and the intervals between his crusades — Ireland, Bulgaria, Ireland again — were devoted, if in opposition, to theology, if in office, to Scrooge-like exercises in Treasury economy. But this ignorance of the masses did not preclude an extraordinary faith in their inherent goodness, in their capacity for righteous wrath, which he contrasted with the selfishness of the classes. And it really was true that at this era of their history, the British masses were susceptible to gusts of outward-looking moral indignation unparalleled before or since, or in any other country. Victorian religious and ethical sensitivity was at its apogee. That Disraeli of all people should have been Prime Minister at this particular moment seems indeed an irony of history . . . .

. . . in an era when royalty still counted for something in politics, the Court was emphatically anti-atrocitarian. The known views of the Queen affected the whole outlook of London society. Queen Victoria's attitude, shared by all her family except the unpopular Duke of Edinburgh who had married a Russian princess, was unequivocally pro-Turk. The Queen had only recently become converted to this view. . . . Gladstone's activities appear to have aroused such indignation in her that, by a process of reaction illogical but not unnatural, she supported the Turks if only because Gladstone denounced them. Disraeli behaved in much the same way. What infuriated the Queen and the

Prime Minister was Gladstone's claim that *realpolitik* should give way to a
moral crusade and that the higher interests of humanity should prevail
95 over 'the permanent and important interests of England', as Disraeli
termed them in his speech at Aylesbury.

The almost pathological animus of the Queen against Gladstone,
which lasted until his dying day, dates from this period. She had indeed
never liked him. He was 'tiresome', 'obstinate', 'tyrannical' and 'tactless'.
100 These are unflattering adjectives, but they are nothing compared with the
language she now began to use in her letters to her favourite child the
Crown Princess of Prussia, which are perhaps the best evidence of her
spontaneous reaction to events. On September 19 she describes his
behaviour as 'most reprehensible and mischievous . . . shameful and
105 unjustifiable'. A week later she refers to 'the disgraceful conduct of that
mischief maker and fire-brand, Mr Gladstone'. By February 1877 he has
become 'that half madman', and henceforth she evidently regarded
insanity as the only explanation of Gladstone's policy.

R. Blake, *Disraeli*, 1966, pp 598–600, 605

Questions

a   Identify Hartington (line 30), Granville (line 39), Rothschilds (line 43), Buckle (line 50).
* b   What were the 'Bulgarian horrors'? How were they associated with the 'Eastern Question'?
c   What does the passage tell us about Gladstone's personality, and about his views on foreign policy?
d   How could Gladstone's intervention in this crisis be viewed pejoratively?
e   '*Realpolitik* should give way to a moral crusade' (lines 93–4). Was this the fundamental difference between Gladstone's and Disraeli's foreign policies?
f   Comment on the reaction of the Queen to Gladstone's pamphlet.

3   Foreign Affairs

(a) Gladstone had never visited Ireland, but for a moment in 1845 he had
felt passionately about the Irish question. He had then deliberately
averted his gaze because other interests engrossed him, and because he
knew his temperament sufficiently well to be at least half-conscious that a
5 mental earthquake would have convulsed his mind if he had permitted it
to dwell upon Ireland. In those circumstances all other interests would
have had to be swept aside. Gladstone considered that his sense of timing
was his most valuable political gift. He noted at the end of his life that the
most 'striking gift . . . entrusted to me . . . is an insight into the facts of
10 particular eras and their relation to one another, which generates in the
public mind a conviction that the materials exist for the formation of a

public opinion and for directing it to a particular end'. He claimed that his proposal of religious equality for Ireland in 1868 was an important illustration of the exercise of that gift; and an entry in his diary (31 December 1868) may have been intended as an explanation of his long neglect of the Irish problem:

> I feel like a man with a burden under which he must fall if he looks to the right or left, or fails from any cause to concentrate mind and muscle upon his progress step by step. This absorption, this excess, . . . is the fault of political life, with its insatiable demands which do not leave the smallest stock of moral energy unexhausted and available for other purposes. . . . Swimming for his life, a man does not see much of the country through which the river winds, and I probably know little of these years through which I work and live.

Gladstone's enemies were prompt to equate the gift for 'right-timing' on which he plumed himself, with opportunism and greed for office. Even his friends were surprised and sometimes amused to find that he always repudiated any suggestion that he was ambitious. Neither friends nor enemies really understood the degree of difference which separated Gladstone from themselves. He was impelled by different motives and guided by different influences and beliefs. Many misunderstandings and disappointments arose from that cause.

Gladstone's opportunism and sense of timing were at the service of a passionate sense of duty. That sense of duty constantly impelled him to devote the great powers which he was well aware that he possessed to purposes which seemed to him to involve the moral issues for the sake of which he had entered politics. In general he was much too fond of the right to be capable of pursuing the expedient, and as a Party leader that was often a disadvantage. Nevertheless there were occasions, particularly towards the end of his life, when he was able to persuade himself that an expedient course was a right one. Whenever that happened Gladstone was visibly troubled, and he was liable unconsciously to discover some preternaturally subtle excuse to which few plain men would have cared to subscribe.

Gladstone's true interests were outside politics, and as he grew older politics disgusted him more and more. He become increasingly anxious to retire and to devote his powers to a defence of the cause of orthodox religion which was being hard-pressed by the rising tide of indifference and by the arrogant assaults of the scientists. When he spoke of his heartfelt desire to withdraw from political life and to possess his soul for a few years before he died, most of his friends and all his enemies believed that he was consciously or unconsciously a hypocrite. They were utterly mistaken, for he was radiantly simple and sincere. Only an overpowering sense of duty, joined to the pressure of his followers, kept him from realizing his longing for retirement until he was aged eighty-four, to the detriment of his reputation and the heartfelt regret of those who knew him best and loved him most.

Because politics were to Gladstone always primarily a duty, while his real interests lay outside them, he failed not only to master the minor political arts, but also to overcome certain faults of temperament which militated against the success of the politics which he advocated with splendid and infectious enthusiasm. He often misjudged individuals because he persistently overrated their goodness and intelligence. He sometimes misjudged events, partly because his prepossessions were so vehement that it was hard for him to be dispassionate, and partly because the subtlety of his intellect was liable to lead him to discover reasons for or against a given cause which were in reality almost worthless.

Once he had convinced himself of the rightness of a cause Gladstone became incapable of moderation . . . .

On 29 December [1878] – his 69th birthday – Gladstone noted: 'Why has my health and strength been so peculiarly sustained. All this year, and more, I think, I have not been confined to bed for a single day. In the great physical and mental effort of speaking, often to large audiences, I have been, as it were, upheld in an unusual manner; and the free and effective use of my voice has been given to me to my own astonishment. Was not all this for a purpose? And has it not all come in connexion with a process to which I have given myself?' He added that this 'appears to me to carry all the marks of the will of God'. It is a great strength to any man, once he has embarked upon a course of action, to believe that he is executing God's will. It is, however, difficult in such circumstances to do justice to the motives of opponents.

Disraeli was irritated by Gladstone's insistence that all important political questions involved clear-cut moral issues. He considered that, in an imperfect world, the choice must lie between policies of varying degrees of expediency. Gladstone considered that men who thought like that were corrupted by the insolence of wealth and privilege; and it was for that reason that he wished to divest himself of both. For the remainder of his life he directed his stormy and emotional appeal over the heads of 'the upper ten thousand' to the moral and religious instincts of the masses.

P. Magnus, *Gladstone*, 1960 edn, pp 190–1, 256–7

(b) He [Disraeli] instinctively lacked sympathy with small nations struggling to be free. Nationalism, the strongest political impulse of his day passed him by, and what he saw of it he disliked. Basically this hostility stemmed from his fundamental creed, the necessity to uphold 'the aristocratic settlement'. Nationalism in his time was essentially a radical force. There were exceptions, Poland and Germany for example; but in most cases national self-determination was tied up with the struggle for land reform and the expropriation of landlords with a different language and religion from those of their peasant tenants.

Britain's parallel to the Balkans was Ireland, and Disraeli saw it. 'Fancy autonomy for Bosnia with a mixed population . . . autonomy for Ireland would be less absurd.' On another occasion he wondered 'whether in the advice which we are asked to give Turkey we are not committing ourselves to principles which are, or which may be soon,

105 matter of controversy in our own country: for instance, the apportionment of local taxation to local purposes and the right of the peasantry to the soil'.

R. Blake, *Disraeli*, 1966, pp 578—9

Questions

a   Why could neither friends nor enemies really understand Gladstone?

* b   What 'moral issues' (line 35) did Gladstone perceive in politics?

c   Why did Disraeli oppose nationalism?

* d   Which of these two statesmen was more realistic in his view of foreign policy?

e   Do these two biographers write sympathetically about their subjects?

* f   In the post–Freudian era what is the importance of knowing a lot about a person's early life?

X   The Liberal Welfare Reforms

Introduction

Is it only thirty years since the introduction of the Welfare State, only fifty years since the end of the workhouses, and only seventy years since the first old-age pensions? That time-span is within the lifetime of many grandparents alive today, and is a reminder of the speed of change in social reform. The origin of these twentieth-century reforms is often said to lie in the period of the Liberal governments, 1905–14, but there is a teleological danger of looking for antecedents to the Welfare State in the decade before the First World War, as a close reading of Briggs and Churchill will indicate.

Recent research on the Liberal reforms stresses the varied influences on social reform and the wider context. For the latter, Dangerfield's and Read's books are strongly recommended: the period of Liberal government was seemingly crisis-ridden, with disputes involving the 1909 budget and reform of the House of Lords, votes for women, trade union militancy, Irish home rule, and Sir Edward Grey's foreign policy. Were the Liberals altruistic in their social policy, were they consciously laying the foundations of a welfare state, or were they vote-catching?

Comparisons of the Liberal reforms with the 1945–51 Labour government's Welfare State, and the treatment of health and poverty in the nineteenth century would be valuable. To what extent did the developing interventionist role of government influence reform? Were the reports of Booth and Rowntree more valuable, or more influential, than reports like the Poor Law Report of 1834? Why, indeed, was there no reform of the Poor Law during the Liberals' period of office?

This final section takes us into the realm of present-day political controversy, and is a useful example of the interaction between the past, the present, and the future: between the events and the evidence, the historian and history's role in society.

Further Reading

R. S. Churchill, *W. S. Churchill, The Young Statesman 1901–1914*, Heinemann, 1967, one volume of a detailed study by the 'official' biographer

G. Dangerfield, *The Strange Death of Liberal England*, Constable, 1936, a controversial interpretation of the crises afflicting the Liberals

* B. B. Gilbert, *The Evolution of National Insurance*, Michael Joseph, 1966, the most useful monograph of the subject

* T. H. Marshall, *Social Policy in the Twentieth Century*, Hutchinson, 1972, sets the Liberal reforms in the context of the century

K. O. Morgan, *The Age of Lloyd George*, Allen and Unwin, 1971, a readable, well-illustrated introduction

E. R. Pike, *Human Documents of the Lloyd George Era*, Allen and Unwin, 1972, well-supplied with documents on the period

D. Read, *Edwardian England*, Historical Association pamphlet, 1972, a brief interpretation, emphasising the growth of tension to 1914

D. Read, *Edwardian England*, Harrap, 1972, a fuller version of the 1972 pamphlet

B. Webb, *Our Partnership*, ed. by B. Drake and M. Cole, Longmans, 1948, offers many insights into the making of social policies from the 'inside'

1   Conditions in York 1901

Labourer. Wages 15s. Received Weekly from other Sources, 2s. 6d. — Total, 17s. 6d.

This household consists of a father, mother, and five children, — four boys aged respectively 11, 9, 7, and 2, and one girl aged 4. The budget extends
5 over a period of twenty-one months, from May 1898 to February 1901. The father is an intelligent man, and interested in Social and Labour questions. He is unable to earn a good wage on account of a physical disability, which was left after a long illness. The mother is a bright, capable little woman, and a good manager; she has had to fight against
10 tremendous odds. She looks underfed and overworked, but is always bright and never complains. Johnnie, the eldest boy, is deformed, and is threatened with tuberculosis, . . . The other children mostly bear some signs of the privations they have so long endured.

The house, which is one of a long row, contains four rooms, and is
15 clean. The door from the street opens into the living-room. There is a pair of lace curtains in the window under which is placed the couch on which Johnnie lies when too ill to go out to play. There is no easy-chair in the room. A table covered with a table-cloth stands back against the wall, on which is placed a fancy box or two and a few books . . . .
20 Mrs R. buys some cheap fresh meat for the Sunday dinner, when the children then have a tiny bit each. During the rest of the week Mrs R. and the children do not have meat for dinner. But the cold meat which is left over from Sunday is saved for Mr R., who takes his dinner with him to work each day. In cold weather the children often have pea soup for
25 dinner, or, if this is not forthcoming, content themselves with bread, dripping, and tea . . . .

When anything extra is wanted for the house the family go short of

food, and if the required expenditure is considerable it is paid off in
weekly instalments. Thus, when Mrs R. bought a mattress, she paid a
certain sum down, and then paid 6d. or 1s. per week until the whole
outlay had been cleared off.

The family get a good many old clothes given to them, which are
carefully repaired, and then probably wear longer than cheap new ones
would do. The father mends the children's boots himself in the evening,
thus effecting a considerable saving.

Mr R. smokes, and buys a weekly paper. He is not a teetotaller, but
'cannot afford to buy beer'. The family spend 5d. weekly upon life
insurance . . . .

Purchases during Week ending June 30, 1899

Friday. — 1½ st. flour, 1s. 10½d.; ¼ st. wheat-meal, 4d.; yeast, 1d.; 1 lb.
butter, 10d.; 2½ lbs. bacon, 1s.; 6 oz. tea, 6d.; 1 lb. currants, 3d.; 1 lb. lard,
4d.; 1¼ lbs. fish, 4d.; 1 tin condensed milk, 5½d.; onions, 1d.

Saturday. — Bag of coal, 1s. 3d.; 4 lbs. beef, 1s. 7½d.; 5 lbs. sugar, 9d.; ½ lb.
dripping, 2½d.; ½ st. potatoes, 2d.; 8 eggs, 6d.; baking powder, 1d.;
literature, 2d.; 1 oz tobacco, 3d.; black lead, 1d.; lemons, 2d.; cabbage,
2d.; insurance, 5d.

Sunday. — Milk, 1d.

Monday. — Stamp, 1d.; stationery, 1d.; sewing-cotton, 2d.; glycerine,
2d.; pair of slippers, 1s. 2½d.; rent, 3s. 3d.

Tuesday. — Yeast, 1d.; 1 lb. soap, 2½d.; starch, 1d.; blacking, 1d.;
scrubbing brush, 3½d.

Thursday. — Lettuce, 1d.

> Seebohm Rowntree, *Poverty. A Study of Town Life*, 1901,
> pp 263–5

Questions

a   How do you think the evidence has been compiled?
b   How effective was the family in spending its weekly income?
*   c   Rowntree applied the terms 'primary' and 'secondary' poverty to
York. What did he mean by these? Which category would suit this
family?
*   d   What social problems were revealed by these studies? In what ways
did the Liberal governments of 1905–14 attempt to solve them?

2 A Welfare State?

The phrase 'welfare state' is of recent origin. It was first used to describe
Labour Britain after 1945 . . . .

The phrase 'welfare state' was seldom defined. It was used to cover both social and economic changes. Among the social changes the demand for more comprehensive social security – 'freedom from want' – was linked, often with little thought, with the demand for greater 'equality of opportunity' through educational reform . . . . There was confusion also on critical issues concerning social change and economic power. The most important economic changes which found a place in British 'definitions' of the 'welfare state' were those which seemed to entail direct and immediate social consequences – the 'abolition of poverty' and the 'conquest of unemployment' . . . .

While political attitudes have been changing not only in Britain but even more markedly in other parts of the world, a small number of British historians and sociologists have begun to make a more searching examination of the 'background' and 'benefits' of the 'welfare state'. As a result of their continuing labours, the significance of each of the great 'turning points' of British 'welfare state' history is already being re-assessed. The stark contrast between the nineteenth and twentieth centuries has been qualified. Landmark legislation such as the National Health Insurance Act of 1911, which hitherto had been treated generally or symbolically, has been re-interpreted in the light of newly discovered or hitherto neglected evidence. The pressures have been more carefully scrutinized, and the setbacks have been examined as well as the successes. Many of the 'reforms' were designed as remedies for specific problems: they were certainly not thought of as contributions to a 'trend' or a 'movement'. The sources of inspiration were multiple – socialism was only one of several strands – and this very multiplicity added to later complications and confusions. The old poor law, from which social services emerged both directly and by reaction, was not so much broken up, as its critics had wished, as eroded away by depression, war, unemployment and the introduction piecemeal of remedial legislation. The social welfare legislation of the Labour government of 1945 – 50, the climax of fifty years of social and political history, has itself begun to be viewed historically. The pre-suppositions which underlay it can now be seen to have been the products of a particular set of circumstances which have already changed. Among those circumstances the experiences of war seems to have been as relevant as the appeal of socialism in determining the practicability and the popularity of introducing comprehensive welfare proposals . . . .

A 'welfare state' is a state in which organized power is deliberately used (through politics and administration) in an effort to modify the play of market forces in at least three directions – first, by guaranteeing individuals and families a minimum income irrespective of the market value of their work or their property; second, by narrowing the extent of insecurity by enabling individuals and families to meet certain 'social contingencies' (for example, sickness, old age and unemployment) which lead otherwise to individual and family crises; and third, by ensuring that all citizens without distinction of status or class are offered the best

50 standards available in relation to a certain agreed range of social services.

The first and second of these objects may be accomplished, in part at least, by what used to be called a 'social service state', a state in which communal resources are employed to abate poverty and to assist those in distress. The third objective, however, goes beyond the aims of a 'social
55 service state'. It brings in the idea of the 'optimum' rather than the older idea of the 'minimum'. It is concerned not merely with abatement of class differences or the needs of scheduled groups but with equality of treatment and the aspirations of citizens as voters with equal shares of electoral power . . . .
60 Long before the Webbs urged the need in 1909 for government action to secure 'an enforced minimum of civilised life', the case for particular minima had been powerfully advocated. Yet the idea of basing social policy as a whole on a public commitment to 'minimum' standards did not become practical politics in Britain until the so-called 'Beveridge
65 revolution' of the Second World War . . . .

[An example for the Liberals was] the social service legislation of the Ballance—Seddon—Reeves ministry in New Zealand from 1891 onwards and . . . the legislation of the Turner government in Victoria from 1895.
70 Much of this legislation was concerned with the creation of effective departments of labour and the control of sweated industries paying low wages to their workers. In both Australia and New Zealand, however, pensions legislation was either introduced or just round the corner by the end of the nineteenth century. The New Zealand Old Age Pensions Act
75 of 1898 was the first in a British dominion. It provided at state expense pensions to people of good character but with little or no means above the age of sixty-five. New South Wales and Victoria followed the example of New Zealand in 1901, and the new federal constitution of Australia stated in the same year that the Commonwealth might legislate for old age and
80 invalid pensions. A federal act of 1908 extended the old age pension system to all Australian states and included also pensions for the blind and for permanently disabled persons. In the same year Britain passed its first non-contributory old age pension act after decades of pressure from philanthropists, societies and even politicians. It was an act hedged round
85 with moral qualifications, but it nonetheless marked, as did dominions legislation, an attempt to get away from the harshness of an all-embracing poor law. 'The state was making new provision for welfare, in piecemeal fashion, outside of and parallel to the poor law.' This, it has been argued, was 'the real beginning of the welfare state in its modern form' . . . .

Asa Briggs, 'The Welfare State in Historical Perspective', in *Archives Européennes de Sociologie*, 2 1961, pp 221–3, 228, 231, 244

Questions

a In what ways was the term 'welfare state' confusing?

b What had research up to 1961 contributed to the debate on the Liberal reforms?

c What distinctions does Briggs draw between a 'welfare state' and a 'social service state'?

* *d* To what extent did Australia and New Zealand provide examples for the 1908 Old Age Pensions Act?

* *e* Do the Liberal social reforms of 1906–14 fit the notion of a 'social service state' better than a 'welfare state'?

* *f* What are the links between the Liberal social reforms of 1906–14 and the Labour reforms of 1945–51?

3 A Liberal Viewpoint

The social machinery at the basis of our industrial life is deficient, ill-organised, and incomplete. While large numbers of persons enjoy great wealth, while the mass of the artisan classes are abreast of and in advance of their fellows in other lands, there is a minority, considerable in
5 numbers, whose condition is a disgrace to a scientific and professedly Christian civilisation, and constitutes a grave and increasing peril to the State . . . .

I agree most whole-heartedly with those who say that in attempting to relieve distress or to regulate the general levels of employment, we must
10 be most careful not to facilitate the very disorganisation of industry which causes distress. But I do not agree with those who say that every man must look after himself, and that the intervention by the State in such matters as I have referred to will be fatal to his self-reliance, his foresight, and his thrift. We are told that our non-contributory scheme of old-age
15 pensions, for instance, will be fatal to thrift, and we are warned that the great mass of the working classes will be discouraged thereby from making any effective provision for their old age. But what effective provision have they made against old age in the past? If terror be an incentive to thrift, surely the penalties of the system which we have
20 abandoned ought to have stimulated thrift as much as anything could have been stimulated in this world. The mass of the labouring poor have known that unless they made provision for their old age betimes they would perish miserably in the workhouse. Ye they have made no provision; and when I am told that the institution of old-age pensions will
25 prevent the working classes from making provision for their old age, I say that cannot be, for they have never been able to make such provision. And I believe our scheme, so far from preventing thrift, will encourage it to an extent never before known.

It is a great mistake to suppose that thrift is caused only by fear; it
30 springs from hope as well as from fear; where there is no hope, be sure there will be no thrift. No one supposes that five shillings a week is a satisfactory provision for old age. No one supposes that seventy is the earliest period in a man's life when his infirmities may overwhelm him.

We have not pretended to carry the toiler on to dry land; it is beyond our power. What we have done is to strap a lifebelt around him, whose buoyancy, aiding his own strenuous exertions, ought to enable him to reach the shore . . . .

The social field lies open. There is no great country where the organisation of industrial conditions more urgently demands attention. Wherever the reformer casts his eyes he is confronted with a mass of largely preventable and even curable suffering. The fortunate people in Britain are more happy than any other equally numerous class have been in the whole history of the world. I believe the left-out millions are more miserable. Our vanguard enjoys all the delights of all the ages. Our rearguard straggles out into conditions which are crueller than barbarism. The unemployed artisan, the casual labourer, and the casual labourer's wife and children, the sweated worker, the infirm worker, the worker's widow, the under-fed child, the untrained, undisciplined, and exploited boy labourer — it is upon these subjects that our minds should dwell in the early days of 1909.

The Liberal Party has always known the joy which comes from serving great causes. It must also cherish the joy which comes from making good arrangements. We shall be all the stronger in the day of battle if we can show that we have neglected no practicable measure by which these evils can be diminished, and can prove by fact and not by words that, while we strive for civil and religious equality, we also labour to build up — so far as social machinery can avail — tolerable basic conditions for our fellow-countrymen . . . .

We have taken a great step already. I must say that he is rather a sour kind of man who can find nothing to notice in the Old-Age Pensions Act except its little flaws and petty defects. . . . No; in spite of Socialistic sneer and Tory jeer and glorious beer, and all the rest of it, I say it is a noble and inspiring event, for which this Parliament will be justly honoured by generations unborn . . . .

There are many political injustices in this country and many absurd, oppressive, or obsolete practices. But the main aspirations of the British people are at this present time social rather than political. They see around them on every side, and almost every day, spectacles of confusion and misery which they cannot reconcile with any conception of humanity or justice. They see that there are in the modern state a score of misfortunes that can happen to a man without his being in fault in any way, and without his being able to guard against them in any way . . . .

. . . in my sincere judgment the British democracy will not give their hearts to any Party that is not able and willing to set up that larger, fuller, more elaborate, more thorough social organisation, without which our country and its people will inevitably sink through sorrow to disaster and our name and fame fade upon the pages of history . . . .

W. S. Churchill, *Liberalism and the Social Problem*, 1909, pp 197–8, 208–10, 235–7

Questions

a   Define 'artisan classes' (line 3), 'non-contributory scheme of old-age pensions' (lines 14–15), 'sweated worker' (line 47).

b   What reasons does Churchill suggest for social change?

c   What is the evidence that Churchill had in mind a 'social service state' rather than a 'welfare state'?

*   d   How did Churchill extend his concern for the industrial worker in 1909?

*   e   The writer makes implicit reference to the 1795 Speenhamland 'system' and the 1834 Poor Law Amendment Act. Does the 1908 scheme mark a new departure, or a return to an old system?

*   f   What reliability can the historian place on political speeches as sources of evidence?

4   In Retrospect

Each of the Liberal reforms had its own specific origins and prehistory. Some historians prefer to see them as individual solutions to particular social problems, not as part of a wider movement. At one level of analysis this is perfectly reasonable. The failure of previous social measures, or the
5   lack of them, combined with exposure and analysis of each social problem, led to the proposal and adoption of new solutions. But 'failure' implies standards against which it is measured, and a political will to achieve success. As Tawney put it, 'the continuance of social evils is not due to the fact that we do not know what is right, but to the fact that we
10   prefer to continue doing what is wrong'.

There were many participants in the creation of the Liberal reforms who had no thought of creating a 'welfare state' of the type which developed in Britain after 1945. Indeed many of the Liberals of 1906–14 would been appalled by the prospect. Moreover the measures adopted
15   always had a tactical significance in the parliamentary struggle between the parties: each was a response to a specific electoral situation, as was the case with the decision to proceed with labour exchanges and unemployment insurance in 1908–9. But this does not mean that social reform can be completely explained in such terms. Key figures, like Lloyd George
20   and Churchill, looked beyond individual pieces of legislation towards the creation of a society in which the worst ravages of poverty would be eliminated. They saw the strategic importance of welfare measures which would, at one and the same time, act as an antidote to socialism and hinder the polarisation of the electorate between Labour and Conservatives in
25   Britain, contribute to the efficiency of the British economy by preventing the physical and mental deterioration of the workers, and provide a measure of social justice which would help to attract working-class votes without alienating the middle classes.

The welfare reforms did not, however, originate exclusively in the

30 heroic vision of a few Liberal individuals. There were other competing proposals for social reform in Britain in the late nineteenth and early twentieth centuries. Liberal Unionists sought to achieve substantially similar results to the Liberals, though by different fiscal and legislative means. The working classes, or rather organisations representing them,
35 also had proposals for social reform which sometimes started from different assumptions and pointed to widely different conclusions. Part of the problem is to explain why the Liberal solutions were adopted; but the more fundamental question is, why were all these various proposals under simultaneous discussion? This is the ultimate justification for
40 concentrating on the common influences on the origins of the reforms.
. . . other societies, facing similar problems, adopted similar measures, and the British social reforms have to be seen in the wider context of the response of capitalist societies to the experience of economic growth . . . .
45 Much more is now known about the influence of economic, political, ideological and institutional changes. The desire to retain as much as possible of the existing capitalist economic system, at a time when it was under increasing pressure from within and without, seems to have been the most important motive in the origins of the Liberal reforms. The
50 'class abatement' aspects, as Marshall called them, were clearest in measures dealing with unemployment. As time passed and other measures to incorporate the working-class leadership into the political establishment took effect, social reform could more readily take the form of concessions to legitimate popular demand. Changing attitudes to
55 poverty, the redefinition of the relationship between the state and its citizens, and improved statistical knowledge also played a part in the process of reform, but humanitarian opinion, by itself, seems to have achieved less than an earlier generation of historians believed . . . .
In the end . . . it will still be necessary to put the reforms back into the
60 context of late Victorian and Edwardian society. It is not sufficient to continue accumulating fragments of knowledge about specific aspects of the reforms. They will have to be related to the other changes in the economy which governments increasingly sought to control. There is a need for a return to the breadth of vision of Halévy and some of his
65 predecessors, who were aware that social reform was only one part of a search for ways of preserving British imperial society.

J. R. Hay, *The Origins of the Liberal Welfare Reforms 1906–14*, 1975, pp 61–3

Questions

a What was the link between party politics and the Liberal social reforms?
b What does Hay regard as the most important motive in the origins of the Liberal reforms?
c What was the 'class abatement' aspect of these reforms?

 d How has research on the Liberal reforms altered in recent years and what does Hay see as the need for future study on the reforms?

* *e* Was there anything new in the Liberals' approach to the problems of social welfare?

* *f* What is the connexion between these reforms and the alleged 'Crisis of Liberal England'?